My Enchanted Island

Norma Iris Pagan Morales

ISBN 978-1-959895-84-8 (paperback)
ISBN 978-1-959895-83-1 (ebook)

Printed in the United States of America

Acknowledgement

This book is dedicated to my loving family, especially my sister Adelin and my father Juan. They are both gone; however, they live very deep in my heart. They were always there when I needed them.

Introduction

FAMILY STORIES

I can only say that we should treasure each moment of our lives. I am sitting here remembering about my childhood. Wow, there are many pleasant memories. Some are gone; however, they live very deep in my heart.

STORIES or TALES

Some of my stories will help my readers realize that life is too short.
Even though this is a recollection of my life and others in my family, it will help young adults relate to their own family ties.
As you begin reading, you will notice that I began with the history of my island. It is not only interesting, but important to know the origin of any individual....

Contents

Chapter 1

Puerto Rico My Enchanted Island

Did you know that Puerto Rico is only a two-hour flight from the continental U.S.? How convenient is that? If you live in the states, you could be on a plane tomorrow to America's Caribbean territory and relax on untouched beaches in no time.

Maybe you'll check the art museums in San Juan and shop at chic boutiques. At night, you could sip piña coladas and salsa dance. Vacationing in Puerto Rico provides you with this and more.

Come and discover the best island in the Caribbean, my Puerto Rico.

San Juan, the bustling capital city, was founded by Spanish colonists in 1521 and is the second-oldest European- founded city in the Americas. It's somewhat crowded with 4 million sanguineous.

But don't let this deter you from exploring the metropolis which mixes modern and colonial architecture.

Just walk around the cobblestone streets of Old San Juan and you'll see UNESCO World Heritage Sites such as the governor's mansion and fortifications.

You must go to El Balneario de Carolina and catch some sun on one of San Juan's best beaches. You may even want to parasail. To immerse yourself in history, head to Castillo San Felipe del Morro, a 16th-century fortress and explore the surroundings.

After that, go to Condado's Avenida Ashford and shop until you drop by designer boutiques.

Your visit to San Juan wouldn't be complete without sailing on San Juan Bay. First, you'll be welcomed aboard and given safety instructions.

You'll also learn the basics of sailing. Next, it's time to set sail for a two-hour sailboat cruise. You'll relax and sip complimentary drinks and eat fresh strawberries or appetizers, extra purchase, as your guide tells you the history of San Juan, share cultural insights.

The perfect waters will mesmerize you and as you look for dolphins, sea turtles and stingrays.

Also, notice various seabirds. Tours are usually limited to six people and make for a more intimate experience.

Grab your raingear and enjoy a half-day trip to the El Yunque rainforest. It's here that you'll find waterfalls, spectacular views, the habitat of Puerto Rico's plants and endangered wildlife, and nature trails. In fact, the 2.6 trail puts you upon the summit at 3,496 feet.

If you want to enhance your hike, go along Forest Road 10 to the Mt. Britton observation tower and climb the spiral staircase that leads to a viewing platform. Bring your camera, so you can take photos to share with family and friends.

When the sun goes down, you don't have to call it a night. Have a kayak adventure on a lagoon at Las Cabezas de San Juan Reserve and you'll see how the water sparkles and shines underneath you.

How does this happen? When your paddle or hand brushes through the water, plankton glows in fluorescent colors, making your water adventure an enchanted experience. You can even swim in the water to make it even more of a magical moment. How cool is that?

The blend of Spanish, Indian and African influences give Puerto Rico an international charm. It's easy to see why Puerto Rico attracts millions of visitors and is called the "Island of Enchantment" by locals.

Not only does the country offer fun in the sun, but it has cool bars and lush rainforests, too. It's the perfect getaway because there's something for everyone. Let's face it, you won't be able to resist the charm of Puerto Rico's adventurous history and tropical land.

When you get tired of the north part of Puerto Rico, come and visit us jibaritos on the south part of the island....

This might sound like an advertisement but is not. I live on this island. I was born in Ponce, and now I live in Mayaguez.

I sometimes get angry because all you hear is about San Juan. The whole island is beautiful. Tourism only concentrates in San Juan. I bet they have never visited our 78 towns. Each town is unique in their own way.

This book will explain everything about my island.

PUERTO RICO!

Chapter 2

Grandma's Stories

My dear "abuelita", Ceferina Figueroa Bellos. She was my mother's mother. She was a very quiet and gentle person. Ceferina was quite a storyteller. She used to tell me many stories about the Taíno Indians and many more.

I remember running to her house every afternoon right after school. Grandma would have a pitcher of lemonade and freshly baked cookies. My brother Julio and I never missed our story hour. It was rather pleasant listening to "abulita's" sweet angelic voice.

Believe me, it was better than any T.V. program. She should have written everything she narrated because they were enjoyable legends for the entire family.

She began each event as followed:

I want you, Normy and Chiqui, to never forget where you came from. It is important to treasure our customs and traditions. Also, I want both of you to pass it on to our future generations.

"Abuelita's" voice was magical. We were transported into the past the minute she began talking…

The Island of Puerto Rico was originally populated by the Taíno Indians. It was claimed in 1493 by Christopher Columbus for the Kingdom of Spain….

The Taíno Indians were divided into two categories:

The Naborias and the Nitaínos

The Naborias were the commoners and the Nitaínos were the nobles. They were governed by male chiefs known as "Caciques". Both groups were advised by priests or healers known as "Bohiques".

The "Caciques"

The "Caciques" liked the privilege of wearing golden pendants called "guanine". They used to live in square "bohíos", instead of the round ones of ordinary villagers. They always sat on wooden stools to be above the guests they received.

Now let's take a look at the "Bohiques"

The "Bohiques" were well respected because of their healing powers. They had the ability to speak with God. The "Bohiques" were consulted and were the only ones to grant the Taíno's permission to engage in important tasks.

The Matrilineal System

The Taíno had a matrilineal system of kinship, descent and inheritance. When a male heir was not present, the inheritance or succession would go to the oldest male child of the deceased's sister.

The Taíno had post-marital residence, meaning a newly married couple lived in the household of the maternal uncle. He was more important in the lives of his niece's children than their biological father.

The uncle introduced the boys to men's societies. Some Taíno practiced polygamy. Men, and sometimes women, might have two or three spouses. A few caciques had as many as thirty wives.

HARD WORKING INDIVIDUALS

The Taíno women

The Taíno women were highly skilled in agriculture.

Those women really had a green thumb. Planting was very important for the whole tribe. Everyone depended on it. The vegetables and fruits were part of their daily meals.

The Taíno men

The men's job was to go fishing and hunting. They made fishing nets and ropes from cotton and palm trees. Bows and arrows were used for hunting. They developed the use of poisons on their arrowheads.

Their dugout canoes were made in various sizes. The canoes were so big that they could hold from two to one hundred and fifty people. An average-sized canoe would hold about fifteen to twenty people.

Hair and clothing style

A frequently worn hair style for women featured bangs in front and longer hair in back. They sometimes wore gold jewelry, paint, and or shells. Taíno men sometimes wore short skirts. Taíno women wore a similar garment after marriage.

Living Quarters

The Taíno lived in settlements called "yucayeques", which varied in size depending on the location. Those in Puerto Rico and Hispaniola were the largest. They had smaller "yucayeques" in the Bahamas.

In the center of a typical village was a central plaza, used for various social activities such as games, festivals, religious rituals, and public ceremonies.

The plazas had many shapes, including oval, rectangular narrow and long. Ceremonies were the deeds of our ancestors. They were called "areitos".

"Areítos" were especially common among the Classic Taíno of Hispaniola and Puerto Rico, but they were held in all Taíno areas. "Areítos" were held for a variety of reasons.

Explanation of the "Areitos"

In the early days of European colonization, Taíno chiefs hosted "areítos" for Spanish visitors, who recorded information about the ceremonies.

According to the historical documentation, "areítos" often featured assemblies of nobles dancing and singing to music played with rattles and drums.

The ceremonies invoked elements of the Taíno culture and religious practice. These practices included worship of the "zemi" and ancestors. "Areítos" were held in designated spaces, specifically the public plaza or dance ground outside the chief's house.

Classic Taíno villages often featured an elaborate dance court, an outdoor area surrounded by earthwork banks and sometimes stone carvings of the zemi.

Often, the general population lived in large circular buildings "bohios", constructed with wooden poles, woven straw, and palm leaves. These houses, built surrounding the central plaza, could hold ten to fifteen families.

The cacique and his family lived in rectangular buildings called "Caney" of similar construction, with wooden porches.

The Taíno's home furnishings included cotton hammocks, " hamacas", sleeping and sitting mats made of palms, wooden chairs "dujo or duh" with woven seats, platforms, and cradles for children.

Caguana Ceremonial ball court or "batey" were outlined with stones. At the "batey" the Taíno played their ceremonial games. Those games on the batey are believed to have been used for conflict resolution between communities.

The most elaborate ball courts are found at chiefdoms' boundaries. Often, chiefs made wagers on the possible outcome of a game.

Those games were very organized. They had opposing teams with ten to thirty players. Each team used a solid rubber ball. Normally, the teams were composed of men, but occasionally women played the game as well.

Arawak Language

The term Arawak originally applied specifically to the South American group who self-identified as Arawak or Lokono. The Taíno Indians spoke Arawak. They did not have written communication.

Arawakan was a term meaning "good" or "noble" that some is used to distinguish their group from the neighboring Island Caribs.

In 1871, ethnologist Daniel Garrison Brinton proposed calling the Caribbean population "Island Arawak". This was due to their cultural and linguistic similarities with the mainland Arawak.

After a while, the scholars shortened this convention to "Arawak", creating confusion between the island and mainland groups.

In the 20th century, scholars such as Irving Rouse resumed using "Taíno" for the Caribbean group to emphasize their distinct culture and language.

These are some Taíno words that have been incorporated into Spanish and English:

Barbacoa-barbecue	hamaca -hammock
kanoa- canoe	tabaco-tobacco
yuca, batata-sweet potato	juracán-hurricane

For warfare, the men made wooden war clubs, which they called "macana". It was about one inch thick and was like the coco macaque. By the way, we still use the word "macana".

Sometimes Mama Nina would explain how the Taínos made their meals. As she explained it, she prepared delicious treats of "casabe".

Taíno ate balanced meals. Their nutrition included vegetables, fruits, meat, and fish. There were no large animals native to the Caribbean, but they captured and ate small animals, such as hutias which are from the rodent's family. The Taíno also ate earthworms, lizards, turtles, and birds.

The Manatees were speared. The fish were caught in nets, speared, trapped in dams, or caught with hook and line. Wild parrots were decoyed with domesticated birds. The iguanas were taken from trees and other vegetation.

The Taíno stored live animals until they were ready to be consumed: fish and turtles were stored in dams, and hutias and dogs were stored in corrals.

Due to this lack of large animals, the Taíno people became very skilled fishermen. One technique was to hook a remora, also known as a suckerfish, to a line secured to a canoe and wait for the fish to attach itself to a larger fish or even a sea turtle.

Once this happened, men would jump into the water and bring in their assisted catch.

Another method used by the Taíno was to take shredded stems and roots of poisonous senna shrubs and throw them into nearby streams or rivers.

Upon eating the bait, the fish were stunned just long enough to allow the fishermen to gather them in. This poison did not affect the edibility of the fish.

Taíno tribesmen, mostly young boys, also collected mussels and oysters in shallow waters and within the mangroves.

Taíno relied a lot on agriculture. Fields for important root crops, such as the staple yuca, were prepared by heaping up mounds of soil, called conucos. This improved soil drainage and fertility as well as delaying erosion, allowing for longer storage of crops in the ground.

Less important crops, such as corn, was raised in simple clearings created by slash and burn technique. Typically, conucos were three feet high and nine feet in circumference and were arranged in rows.

When I was young, my great grandmother told me to be careful if I was going to prepare yucca or cassave. If those root vegetables were not prepared properly, they could be hazardous to your health. My ancestors learned from the Taínos....

Their primary root crop was yucca or cassave which is a woody Shrub cultivated for its edible and starchy roots. It was planted using a coa, a kind of hoe made completely from wood.

Women processed the poisonous variety of cassava by squeezing it to extract the toxic juices. Then they would grind the roots into flour for baking bread. Batata, sweet potato, was the next most important root crop.

Contrary to mainland practices, corn was not ground into flour and baked into bread but was cooked and eaten off the cob. Corn bread becomes moldy faster than cassave bread in the high humidity of the Caribbean.

Corn was also used to make an alcoholic beverage known as chicha.

The Taíno grew squash, beans, peppers, peanuts, and pineapples. Tobacco, calabashes, West Indian pumpkins, cotton were grown around the houses.

Other fruits and vegetables, such as palm nuts, guavas, and Zamia roots, were collected from the wild.

Our Taíno Indians were very friendly and humble. Their peaceful life and daily tasks changed when the Spaniard claimed it....

Chapter 3

Spaniards in Puerto Rico 1493–1898

My Grandma Ceferina was born on August 26, 1900; therefore, she grew up under the American ruling. She told my brother Julio and me many stories related to the Spaniards and the Taínos. We saw how sad she got when she was trying to remember all the incidents that happened during that era....

Ceferina, called by all her grandchildren, "Mama Nina" was very knowledgeable about the history of our island. Her parents were from Spain.

They had many properties throughout the island. Mama Nina never went to Spain, but her parents traveled often.

I miss Mama Nina's stories when we moved to New York, however, she used to go to New York for short visits.

Julio and I were very excited every afternoon after school. We were ready to listen to her story about the Spaniards. She began as always, asking about our day. It was so different living in New York. So, it was great having our "abuelita" in our house.

I forgot to mention that we were celebrating Hispanic heritage month in school. The stories that Mama Nina told us were very educational and important.

All the students in my class were selected to perform on Puerto Rico discovery Day. Mama Nina helped me and guess what? My class won first prize for best performance thanks to Mama Nina....

Mama Nina began her story in a very different and strange tone. Her stories were somewhat sad.

When Columbus arrived in Puerto Rico during his second voyage on November 19, 1493, the island was inhabited by the Taíno Indians. They called it Borikén; Borinquen in Spanish translation.

Columbus named the island San Juan Bautista, in honor of the Catholic saint, John the Baptist.

After reporting the findings of his first travel, Columbus brought with him, this time, a letter from King Ferdinand. It was empowered by a papal that authorized any course of action necessary for the expansion of the Spanish Empire and the Christian faith.

It was Juan Ponce de León, a lieutenant under Columbus, who founded the first Spanish settlement, Caparra, on August 8, 1508. He later served as the first governor of Puerto Rico.

Eventually, traders and other maritime visitors came to refer to the entire island as Puerto Rico, and San Juan became the name of the main trading and shipping port.

At the beginning of the 16th century, the Spanish people began to colonize the island. Despite the Laws of Burgos of 1512 and other decrees for the protection of the indigenous population, some Taíno Indians were forced into an encomienda system of forced labor in the early years of colonization.

Mama Nina explained everything as if she was our history teacher....

Let's look at the "Encomienda System"

The encomienda was a dependency relation system that started in Spain during the Roman Empire. It really meant that the stronger people protected the weakest in exchange for a service.

It was later used during the Spanish colonization of the Americas and the Philippines. The Spanish monarch would assign a Spaniard with the task of "protecting" a specific group of Native Americans.

In the encomienda, the Spanish crown granted a person a specified number of natives of a specific community, with the indigenous leaders in charge of mobilizing the assessed tribute and labor.

In turn, "encomenderos" were to take responsibility for instruction in the Christian faith, protection from warring tribes and pirates, instruction in the Spanish language and development and maintenance of infrastructure.

In return, the natives would give tributes in the form of metals, maize, wheat, pork, or any other agricultural product.

During the first decade of the Spanish presence in the Caribbean, the Spaniards were divided. The natives, who in some cases worked tirelessly, and the Spaniards who came after the dismissal of Christopher Columbus.

The Spanish crown sent a royal governor, Fray Nicolás de Ovando, who established the formal encomienda system. In many cases, natives were forced to do hard labor and subjected to extreme punishment and death if they resisted.

Queen Isabella of Castile had forbidden Indian slavery and deemed the indigenous "free vassals of the crown," allowing many natives and Spaniards to appeal to the Real Audiencias.

Encomiendas were often characterized by the geographical displacement of those enslaved and the breakup of communities and family units, but the encomienda in Mexico functioned to rule these free vassals of the crown via existing community hierarchies, with the indigenous not forced permanently from their families, homes, and land.

In the former Inca Empire, for example, the system continued the Inca and even pre-Inca traditions of extracting tribute in the form of labor.

By the time Queen Isabella came to help the Taínos, it was too late. The Taíno Indians were suffering extremely high fatalities from epidemics of the Europeans.

The Taíno became nearly extinct as a culture following settlement by Spanish colonists, primarily due to infectious diseases to which they had no immunity. The first recorded smallpox outbreak in Hispaniola occurred in December 1518 and January 1519.

The 1518 smallpox epidemic killed 90% of the natives who had not already perished. Warfare and harsh enslavement by the colonists had also caused many deaths.

By 1548, the native population had declined to fewer than 500. Starting in about 1840, there have been attempts to create a quasi-indigenous Taíno identity in rural areas of Cuba, the Dominican Republic, and Puerto Rico.

This trend accelerated among the Puerto Rican community in the United States in the 1960's.

When Mama Nina finished her story, we asked her why she was so sad. She explained that when the Spaniards claimed Puerto Rico, no one could even mention the Indians. It was an insult just being part Taíno...

Chapter 4

Enslaved Africans in Puerto Rico

The enslaved Africans had already begun to compensate for the Indian labor loss, but their numbers were proportionate to the diminished commercial interest Spain soon began to demonstrate for the island.

The history of Puerto Ricans of African descent begins with the immigration of African free men called "libertos", who accompanied the invading Spanish Conquistadors.

The Spaniards enslaved the Taínos, the native inhabitants of the island. Many of them died because of Spaniards' oppressive colonization efforts. This presented a problem for Spain's royal government, which relied on slavery to staff their mining and fort-building operations.

Spain's "solution" was to import enslaved West Africans. As a result, most of the African peoples who entered Puerto Rico did so because of the forced migration of the Atlantic slave trade, coming from many different societies of the African continent.

When the gold mines in Puerto Rico were declared exhausted, the Spanish Crown no longer held Puerto Rico as a high colonial priority. It was used as a military base to support naval vessels.

Africans from British and French possessions in the Caribbean were encouraged to migrate to Puerto Rico, thereby providing a population base to support the Puerto Rican quarters.

The Spanish decree of 1789 allowed the slaves to earn or buy their freedom; however, this did little to help their situation. The expansion of sugar cane plantations drove up demand for slaves and their population increased dramatically.

Throughout the years, there were many slave revolts on the island. Slaves who were promised their freedom joined the 1868 uprising against Spanish colonial rule in what is known as the "Grito de Lares".

On March 22, 1873, slavery was abolished in Puerto Rico. The contributions of ethnic Africans to the music, art, language, and heritage have been instrumental to Puerto Rican culture.

Other islands, driven by the markets of intense agricultural, such as Cuba, Saint-Domingue, and Guadeloupe attracted the trade on slave more often than Puerto Rico. In those places, colonists had developed large sugar plantations with the capital to invest in the Atlantic slave trade.

The colonial administration relied heavily on the industry of enslaved Africans and creole-Blacks. They used them for public works and defenses primarily in coastal ports and cities. Those were the small colonial population that had squatted down.

The minor colonial population had no significant industries or large-scale agricultural productions. However, they had enslaved, and free communities lodged around the few coastal settlements, particularly around San Juan. They were also forming lasting Afro-creole communities.

In the meantime, in the island's interior, something was in the works. That is where a developed mixed and independent group began. The whole island relied on them.

They helped keep economy alive. This mostly unsupervised population supplied villages and settlements with food. This group of people was very smart indeed. They set the pattern for what later would be known as the Puerto Rican "Jíbaro" culture.

By the end of the 16th Century, the Spanish Empire was increasing raids from European competitors, the colonial administration throughout the Americas fell into a "bunker mentality."

What is a "bunker mentality"? It is an attitude of extreme defensiveness and self-justification based on an often-exaggerated sense of being under persistent attack from others.

At this point, the Spaniards had to use imperial strategists and urban planners. They had to redesigned port settlements into military posts with the objective of protecting Spanish territorial claims. Also, they had to safeguard the safe passing of the king's silver-laden Atlantic Fleet to the Iberian Peninsula.

San Juan, at this time, served as an important port-of-call for ships drove across the Atlantic by its powerful trade winds. West Indies convoys linked Spain to the island, sailing between Cádiz and the Spanish West Indies.

The colony's seat of government sat on the forested Island of San Juan and for a time became one of the most heavily fortified settlements in the Spanish Caribbean. San Juan earned the name of the "Walled City."

Why "Walled City"?

Nicknames for San Juan:
"La Ciudad Amurallada"--Spanish for
"The Walled City"

"Ciudad Capital"
Spanish for "Capital City"

The Spaniard put many forts to protect the city…

Today, the island still has various forts and walls, such as La Fortaleza, Castillo San Felipe del Morro, and Castillo San Cristóbal. They were designed to protect the people and the Port of San Juan from the raids of the Spanish European competitors.

In 1625, in the Battle of San Juan, the Dutch commander Boudewijn Hendricksz tested the defenses' limits like no one else. He learned from

Francis Drake's previous failures. He also avoided the cannons of the castle of San Felipe Del Morro.

Hendricksz quickly entered his seventeen ships into the San Juan Bay. Then, he occupied the port and attacked the city while the people hurried for shelter behind the Morro's ditch and high walls.

Many Historians consider this event the worst attack on San Juan. Though the Dutch set the village on fire, they failed to conquer the Morro, and its batteries pounded their troops and ships until Hendricksz believed the cause lost.

Hendricksz's expedition eventually helped push protection for the whole island. There were constructions of defenses for the San Cristóbal Hill. Puerto Rico was really under strict rules.

The people and administration were soon ordered to prevent the landing of invaders away from the Morro's artillery. Urban planning responded to the needs of keeping the colony in Spanish hands.

During the late 16th and early 17th centuries, Spain concentrated its colonial efforts on the more prosperous mainland North, Central, and South American colonies. With the introduction of the lively Bourbon Dynasty in Spain in the 1700s, the island of Puerto Rico began a gradual shift to more imperial attention.

More roads began connecting previously isolated inland settlements to coastal cities. The coastal settlements like Arecibo, Mayaguez, and Ponce began acquiring importance of their own, separated from San Juan.

By the end of the 18th century, merchant ships from different groups or nationalities threatened the tight regulations of the Mercantilist system. It turned each colony solely toward the European metropole and limited contact with other nations.

U.S. ships came to surpassed Spanish trade and with this also came the exploitation of the island natural resources. Slavers, which had made but few stops on the island before, began selling more of its enslaved Africans to growing sugar and coffee plantations.

The increasing number of Atlantic wars in which the Caribbean islands played major roles, like the Jenkin's Ear, the Seven Years, and the Atlantic Revolutions, ensured Puerto Rico's growing esteem in Madrid's eyes.

By the time when independence movements in the larger Spanish colonies gained success, new waves of loyal creole immigrants began arriving in Puerto Rico. They helped tilt the island's political balance toward the crown.

In 1809, to secure its political bond with the island and during the European Peninsular War, the Supreme Central Junta based in Cádiz recognized Puerto Rico as an overseas province of Spain.

It gave the island residents the right to elect representatives to the recently assembled Spanish parliament Cádiz Cortes, with equal representation to mainland Iberian, Mediterranean Balearic Islands and Atlantic maritime Spanish provinces Canary Islands.

Now, let's look at some important people which helped the island be recognized in many ways...

Ramón Power y Giralt

Who was Ramón Power y Giralt?

Captain Ramón Power y Giralt
October 7, 1775 – June 10, 1813

He was commonly known as Ramón Power. According to the Puerto Rican historian, Lidio Cruz Monclova, he was also among the first native-born Puerto Ricans to refer to himself as a "Puerto Rican".

Power fought for the equal representation of Puerto Rico in front of the parliamentary government of Spain. Ramón Power y Giralt, the first Spanish parliamentary representative from the island of Puerto Rico, died after serving a three-year term in the Cortes.

These parliamentary and constitutional reforms were in force from 1810 to 1814, and again from 1820 to 1823. They were twice reversed during the restoration of the traditional monarchy by Ferdinand VII.

Immigration and commercial trade reforms in the 19th century increased the island's ethnic European population and economy. It also expanded Spanish cultural and social imprint on the local character of the island.

Minor slave revolts had occurred in the island throughout the years. One revolt planned and organized was by Marcos Xiorro in 1821.

Marcos Xiorro, an African slave, planned and conspired to lead a slave revolt against the sugarcane plantation owners and the Spanish Colonial government in Puerto Rico.

Although the conspiracy was unsuccessful, he achieved legendary status among the slaves and is part of Puerto Rico's folklore.

During the four centuries of Spanish rule, the island's cultural and physical landscape was transformed. This was the time when the European knowledge, customs, and traditions were introduced.

Roman Catholicism and the Spanish language were the most important characteristic of that special era...

In 1898, following the Spanish American War, Spain ceded the island to the United States under the terms of the Treaty of Paris....

Chapter 5

The Melting Pot of the Caribbean

Why is Puerto Rico sometimes called the melting pot of the Caribbean?

Puerto Rico is a tropical island with diverse ethnic backgrounds. We can say that it is the melting pot of the Caribbean.

For example, the French, Dutch, Irish, Italian, and British were among the so many that tried to conquer this heavenly place.

They left; however, their cultures blended with the ones already existing in the island.

What is the Caribbean?

I can only describe the Caribbean as heaven on earth. It is a paradise filled with beautiful beaches, wonderful and friendly people. The history of this paradise is amazing...

My favorite island in the Caribbean is Puerto Rico. Why Puerto Rico because it is the place where I was born. I am proud of my unique mixture of cultural antecedents.

Regardless of our multi-ethnic composition, the culture held in common by most Puerto Ricans is referred to as mainstream Puerto Rican culture. It is also a Western culture largely derived from the traditions of Western European immigrants.

This all began with the early Spanish settlers, along with other Europeans arriving later such as the Corsicans, Irish, Germans, French, and the West African culture which has been influential.

The majority of Puerto Ricans regard themselves as being of mixed Spanish-European descent. Recent DNA sample studies have concluded that the three largest components of the Puerto Rican genetic profile are in fact indigenous Taíno, European, and African.

At the present time, Puerto Rico is a United States territory located in the northeastern Caribbean. It includes a main island and several tiny islands.

The capital and largest city is San Juan. The territory does not observe daylight saving time, and its official languages are Spanish, which is predominant, and English...

PUERTO RICO TODAY

Puerto Ricans are natural-born citizens of the United States. Puerto Rico does not have a vote in the U.S. Congress, which governs the territory with full jurisdiction under the Puerto Rico Federal Relations Act of 1950. As a U.S. territory, American citizens residing on the island are "disenfranchised at the national level" and may not vote for the President and Vice President of the United States.

However, the territory operates under a local constitution, allowing its citizens to elect a governor.

A 2012 referendum showed a majority 54% of the electorate disagreed with "the present form of territorial status," with full statehood as the preferred option among those who voted for a change of status.

Following this vote, the Legislative Assembly of Puerto Rico enacted a concurrent resolution to request the President and the Congress of the United States to end the status and to begin the process to admit Puerto Rico to the Union as a State. As of 2016, Puerto Rico remains a commonwealth of the United States.

Chapter 6

The Birth

At approximately 10:30 p.m. on Friday, January 15, 1949, Guadalupe and her mother, Dolores, were enjoying a pleasant breeze, when suddenly; they heard Digna from afar....

Guadalupe looked and at her mother and said, "Ya llego la hora que tanto esperabamos". Even though Guadalupe just gave birth to Vicente Pagan my youngest uncle, she was very anxious to assist her mother with the birth of her first grandchild.

They got up from their chairs and walked very fast to Digna's room. Digna was young and healthy; however, she was very nervous because this was going to be her first born.

She asked for her husband, but he was at a wake of one of their neighbors that had died on that day.

Mama Dolores, a licensed midwife, had delivered lots of children; but this child was different because it was going to be her great grandchild.

Both females prepared the room to welcome the baby. Digna wasn't afraid because she knew that Guadalupe and Dolores were ready. Both had the experience and were on duty 24/7 to help in the community before the doctor could make any house call.

Guadalupe sat next to Digna and while holding her hand, she kept telling her stories about all nine babies she had given birth and her last one was just two months old.

With stories and plenty of loving care, it only took Digna about two hours to give birth to a gorgeous baby girl, Norma Iris Pagan Morales.

Mama Dolores was tired but couldn't resist holding her great granddaughter. The baby was cleaned and placed next to her "Mamí".

Digna couldn't believe that this beautiful little creature was her daughter. Her husband Juan came running into the room and started to cry when he saw his wife and their daughter.

The following day, a doctor came to check the mother and child. They were in excellent condition. The newborn weighed 8 pounds and was 19 inches long. The doctor jotted down the exact time, date, and birth of the baby.

He made sure that he had all the necessary information to be documented on the birth certificate...

Digna and Juan decided to name the baby Norma because at that time a very popular soap opera "Norma" that was heard on the radio throughout Puerto Rico. The middle name "Iris" because those eyes glowed with such beauty just as a rainbow after rain.

I was welcomed by nine aunts and uncles. So, I, Norma Iris Pagán Morales, was the luckiest baby. I am the first grandchild on my father's side. My mother's huge family was also present on the day I arrived.

My parents have been living with my grandparents since they got married. Now with my birth, they must think about getting their own place.

They were living with my grandparents because my father and grandfather were in the National Guard. My mother didn't want to be alone while my dad was serving his country.

When my grandmother heard that my parents were planning on moving, she began to cry. She wanted to add an extra room to her house because she was getting so used to me.

Every morning, my grandmother used to take care of my youngest uncle Villen and me. My mother didn't mind. Everyone had their chores in that big happy family.

My father was very firm with his decision to move to his own house. My grandparents had mixed emotions. They were sad, but at the same time happy for the young couple.

Since my father used to work with engineers, he had no problem getting blueprints and permits to build. Let me also mention that my dad was also a licensed plumber and electrician.

A couple of weeks after I was born, my father and his friends started building a house right next to my grandparents.

When the house was finished, they had a big family reunion. It was a double celebration because my mother's family came not only to see us, but also to congratulate my parents on their new house. It was an all-day festivity for both the Pagán and the Morales family.

My mother was very happy with me and enjoyed decorating her very own house. I was a good baby. Every month my mom took me to the doctor for a routine checkup.

When I was six-month-old, the doctor told my parents that I was ready to give up the maternal milk.

My grandfather used to visit us every afternoon. He also sang to me. I enjoyed it very much. That is what I was told of course....

When I was about two years old, my mother started getting morning sickness. She went to the doctor and was informed that she was one month pregnant. She was very happy because I was growing too fast and needed a brother or sister to play.

My father was very happy when he heard the news; however, he told my mother that he hoped that it would be a boy.

My grandfather got very excited when he found out that he was going to be a grandfather once again. He went to the local bar and bought drinks for everyone. Papá Julio didn't care if it was a boy or girl. He just wanted a healthy grandchild.

Chapter 7

Father and Son fighting
for the Same Cause

In the early spring, in 1950, The National Guard Army was training every soldier harder than ever. Everyone knew that soon the National Guard would be mobilized.

My mother and grandmother were sad during those days because they knew that every member in my family would be deployed to Korea.

Since my mother was pregnant with her second child, she was too big to work around the house.

My grandmother, Guadalupe, let her rest because my mother was due soon. This time, both my grandmother Guadalupe and my great-grandmother had a bad feeling about this child.

My mother was always too tired and didn't want to eat. I guess my mom was always sick because she didn't see my father often enough.

On October 20, 1950, my mother went into labor for more hours than expected. She gave birth to another baby girl, my sister Adelin.

My grandmother Lupe and great grandma Dolores were happy because the baby was small, but healthy.

My mother wanted to know if my father was around. My father and grandfather were doing drill at Lucille Field base known today as Fort Allen in Juana Diaz, Puerto Rico.

Both my father and grandfather were happy because the new baby was doing well. They both wanted to go home, but all passes were denied.

My father got very angry. He just wanted an hour to pass to see his wife and daughter. The answer from the commander was no....

My father decided to jump the fence...

So, when his unit went on break, he started walking very fast. There were sugar cane fields and farms before reaching the main road.

As soon as he reached the street, a car stopped and to my father's surprise, it was his commander. The commander looked at him and told him to get in the car. My father was surprised because he was escorted to Ponce to see my mother and my sister.

The commander told him to stay the rest of the evening, but to return to the base the following day. My mother was very happy to see him. Adelin and I were beside my mom when my dad arrived.

The whole family had a wonderful night together.

During the months that followed, things were very rough. Lots of soldiers were sent to Korea. My grandfather and my father were waiting for their orders...

Our nation was facing one of the worst times of that era. Puerto Rico was waiting and willing to fight in Korea. I am proud to say, that my father, CSM Juan José Pagán Rodriguez, of the Puerto Rico National Guard and my grandfather, Staff Sergeant Julio Pagán Torres, now deceased, were among those brave soldiers fighting for our country in one of the bloodiest conflicts.

In order to understand the commotion that was going on in the states and Puerto Rico, I will give you some facts of what our soldiers were facing during that time....

On July 1, 1950, the Army's 24th Infantry Division became the first U.S. troop to arrive in Korea. They were transferred from Japan passing through the Port of Pusan.

The troops took up Positions in Taejon, about 75 miles south of Seoul. A couple of days later on July 19, 1950, the 25th Infantry arrived followed by the 1ˢᵗ Marine Brigade and the 2ⁿᵈ Infantry Division in late July.

Things were getting worse in Korea that on July 20, 1950, the casualties were increasing. More than 2,400 men or 30% were reported dead. Taejon fell under the arms of the enemy.

All Americans and the rest of world were alarmed. This meant that many were going to be called to serve their country. The Reserves and the National Guard will be mobilized.

Puerto Rico, a beautiful island located in the Caribbean, and a Commonwealth of the United States, was getting ready. There was no cultural or language barrier holding those brave men.

Those "Boricuas" were well trained. Three members of my family were in the National Army Guard. They knew that it wouldn't be long for the guard to be call for active duty.

All three were ready to serve their nation. They were Staff Sgt. Julio Pagan Torres, my grandfather, assigned to 65ᵗʰ Infantry 4 machine gun 30 calibers, Sgt. Juan J. Pagan Rodriguez, my father, assigned to 65ᵗʰ Infantry Heavy Mortal Co. and the youngest, my uncle, Cpl. Julio Pagan Rodríguez was assigned to Artillery.

By early September, the new troops were combat ready in hardened fighting units. The Puerto Rican National Guard was mobilized on September 10, 1950. Every "Boricua's" family was worried because their loved ones will leave to an unknown land. Many have never been abroad. Now, they must face a lot of hardships.

It didn't take long for a humble family in Ponce to hear the worst news ever. Their sons and husbands must report for duty. This was awful because all three soldiers were assigned to infantry or artillery.

The women were devastated when they heard the news on the radio. Staff Sgt. Julio Pagan Torres and Sgt. Juan J. Pagan Rodriguez received their orders. Their unit, the 65ᵗʰ Infantry was being mobilized. Cpl. Julio Pagan Rodriguez wasn't called at this time.

The 65th Infantry was now divided. That meant father and son were separated. The 296 Infantry was sent to Tortuguero. They were divided into two groups, 2nd to Juana Diaz and the 3rd to Cayey.

Chapter 8

Waiting for the Worst

Everything was moving too fast. The Puerto Rico National Guard was giving orders left and right. There was no question asked. It didn't matter if there were one sole survivor in a family. Men were needed to go abroad and fight for their country.

Sgt. Juan J. Pagán Rodriguez was ready to fight; however, he had a young wife and two young children. Sgt. Julio Pagán Torres had also young ones. They had a big problem. There was also a possibility that Cpl. Julio Pagán Rodriguez might be called for active duty. They wanted to serve, but they had a family.

The following day, both father and son decided to speak to their commander. The commander found it quite unusual for members of the same family to be called to active duty.

He listened to their petition and wrote all the information given by my father and grandfather. He told Sgt. Juan Pagán Rodriguez that he was the one chosen to go to Korea and that Sgt. Julio Pagán Torres would stay in Puerto Rico.

What follows, will not only put you in tears, but will make you wonder.

In November 1950, Sgt. Juan J. Pagán Rodriguez said goodbye to his beloved wife and family. He was only 22 years old but was fully aware of his commitment. His father promised him that he would take care of the whole family. Sgt. Juan J. Pagán Rodriguez just said, "Bendición Papito" and got on the bus…

Many "Boricuas" were also leaving Puerto Rico. This was the saddest day for the whole island. Saying goodbye was very hard. The 65th Infantry had already sent soldiers to Korea.

Those first infantry soldiers made history throughout the nation. They were known as "The Borinqueneers" The 65th Infantry Regiment started the assault on January 31, 1951.

NO WORD FROM SGT JUAN PAGAN RODRIGUEZ

The Pagán family was very confused during this crisis because right after Sgt. Juan J. Pagán Rodriguez left Puerto Rico, his father Staff Sgt. Julio Pagán received new orders. These orders stated that he was leaving for Korea in December 1950.

This was the worst Christmas gift that anyone could receive. Now Staff Sgt. Julio Pagán Torres was also leaving his family. He told his wife, Guadalupe, "No te apures, todo va a salir bien".

He couldn't face his daughter-in-law, Digna. She was holding her youngest daughter Adelin. Digna was too upset to say goodbye. Sgt. Juan J. Pagán Rodriguez left the island months before and no one knew his whereabouts.

The so many visits to the Red Cross were made in vain. Sgt. Julio Pagán Torres even went to his commander for an answer of his previous visit. The commander apologized for the awful mess and stated that he was sorry.

Sgt. Pagán Torres asked about the previous order. The commander could only say that they were revoked because they got to Washington too late. Communication was very slow in those days…….

ILL FEELINGS IN THE FRONT LINES

Sgt. Juan J. Pagán Rodriguez was already fighting in the front lines. He got to Korea in January 1951 and at this point he was uneasy. He had been away from his family for nearly two months and no news was received.

It was hard to get anything where he was stationed. His new acquired family was his buddies, fellow "BORICUAS". All of them were waiting for some kind of news from Puerto Rico.

In Ponce, Puerto Rico, things weren't that great. With the breadwinner gone, it wasn't easy to raise all those children. Guadalupe and Digna had to go to the Red Cross.

They wanted to hear news from their husbands. The Red Cross assured them that both father and son were fine. Food and emergency money were provided. Digna was worried because the youngest daughter was very ill. Adelin was a very fragile child and needed medical attention.

When the Red Cross saw the baby, they referred her to the best doctors. The child was well taken care of and recovered within months.

By the end of February, troops were sent to the front lines once again.....

IN KOREA

One morning, Sgt. Juan Jose Pagán Rodriguez was ordered to take a couple of guys to a designated area. Sgt. Pagán Rodriguez briefed his men and started walking. It was a cold bitter day and there was a lot of snow on the ground.

The young soldiers were still trying to get used to that weather. They were all melancholy because they missed their sunny and warm Puerto Rico.

Many had suffered from frost bites. It wasn't easy keeping those soldiers motivated. They haven't heard anything from their families in months.

As they were walking, Sgt. Pagán Rodriguez started telling funny stories. The soldiers felt at ease. They reached their destination point. There were many wounded and others were suffering from the cold. Sgt. Pagán Rodriguez and his Troop relieved those men.

The fire never stopped. Sgt. Pagán Rodriguez has been in his post for nearly a week. He was hungry and so were his men. They needed clean uniforms and chow.

Sgt. Juan J. Pagán Rodriguez kept fighting even though he didn't receive any news from Puerto Rico.

Suddenly, he received a message. He was ordered to report to his Commander. The young sergeant was surprised, but at the same time was happy to take a shower and change his uniform.

He was escorted to his superior and to his surprise there was Staff Sergeant Julio Pagán Torres waiting for him.

Words couldn't describe the emotion that those two human beings were feeling. Tears of joy were rolling down their faces. Sgt. Pagán Rodriguez asked his father about the family. He was also puzzled and questioning his father's arrival...both....in Korea...

The Commander of the 65th Infantry told both father and son that they would have to wait for new orders. He also told them that they will leave for Puerto Rico soon....

Those orders never came. Sgt. Juan J. Pagán Rodriguez was once again separated from his father......

A couple of days have gone by....

Sgt. Juan J. Pagán Rodriguez and his men were going to another camp site.

They had a couple of jeeps with plenty of supplies. Sgt. Pagán Rodriguez saw a troop right in front of him. They were going to the same unit.

At that point, Sgt. Juan Pagán Rodriguez got the surprise of his life. His father, Staff Sgt. Julio Pagán Torres was among those men! He called his father and both rode on the same jeep.

Once they arrived at their designated area, their new commandant called them. This time he gave them written orders. That was the best news Sgt. Pagán Rodriguez had received. He was going home, and his father was going with him safe and sound.

Sgt. Pagán Rodriguez and Staff Sgt. Julio Pagán Torres didn't want to be part of the big reception that was waiting for them in Puerto Rico.....

They were the first father and son wearing the same uniform and fighting for the same cause, but they just wanted to see their family.

They went to Ponce without being noticed. A taxi driver was the only witness when they reached home. There were a few gathered in front of the house. None of them were aware that a taxi had stopped there.

The two sergeants got out of the taxi very quietly and opened the gate. Digna and Guadalupe started running once they saw them. It was a great day for the Pagán Family.

Staff Sergeant Julio Pagán Torres and Sergeant Juan J. Pagán Rodríguez were the first father and son to serve the nation. They were in combat together and together returned home to Puerto Rico.

The Korean War brought Puerto Rican soldiers their greatest visibility, highest awards, and most punishing losses.

There were 43, 434 Puerto Ricans in this war and 39, 591 of them were volunteers.

The 65th Infantry was chosen to guard the nation. They received awards for their bravery. It was also the last group of soldiers to leave the combat zone...

Some bullets were whizzing by them as they boarded the ship to evacuate.......

For that a great SALUTE TO OUR "BORICUA" Korean's Heroes. We will never forget them.

CSM Juan J. Pagán Rodriguez was very proud of being a soldier during the Korean Conflict...

CSM JUAN J. PAGAN RODRIGUEZ

MY HERO

In choosing of becoming an NCO…
You accepted many responsibilities
In choosing of becoming a father…
You accepted many responsibilities
You are a role model, a trainer, and a loving father…

As I sit here, thoughts of yesteryears come to mind…
You my father and the soldier…
Dealing with your family
Dealing with your troop…
Both tasks closely related and hard
An Army Non-Commissioned Officer and a father
Of four…
Your wisdom of many years made you a great leader…
Your wisdom of many years made you the father you are…
I salute you dear father…
I salute you for all the years
You devoted to us and to our nation…
May God bless you…
And May God blesses America always!

JUAN J. PAGAN RODRIGUEZ

You were one of the first I laid eyes on when I was born…
I didn't know you at first, but you were my
daddy and later to become my hero…
You were one of the first I loved, and I chose
you over my stuffed animals….

I loved how you'd picked me up…You lift me with one
arm way above your head and I flew like a bird…
As I started to grow, you taught me to stand and walk.
You guided me so carefully so I wouldn't fall.
Once I began to walk on my own, you stood close by
just in case I fell…If I did, you would pick me
up Wipe the tears off my face and kiss my pain away…
Once I got older, I didn't need your help
Walking, but I needed your love and time. We played baseball
and if I couldn't run the bases, you'd lift me up so I could
… Making me feel like I was number one always….
You taught me how to fight and not be afraid of anyone.
You helped me buy my first car in my price range and
you also showed me how to change the tires…
I was the only one of my friends that knew how...
You would do almost anything to see me happy…
You always encouraged me to try my best.
You supported me one hundred and ten percent…
I've come to realize that I'm a lot like you
You helped me realize that common sense isn't that common
You also taught me to be witty
I followed in your steps of being smart
You taught me how to deal with people and how to get
what I wanted….And whenever someone said: You're
just like your dad I couldn't help but smile…
You're not only my dad, but you're my hero…

I remember the many nights you stayed up
late helping me with my schoolwork
I hated math, but you made algebra and geometry so simple…
I'm grown up now, however, I still need your loving bear hugs,

And your encouraging words of wisdom.
Don't forget that I will always be your little girl
And you will always be my loving father and hero
I love you DAD

Chapter 9

The Christening

In October 1952, the Pagán Family was celebrating once again. My father and grandfather had returned from Korea safe. Also, many of their close friends were among those heroes serving during the Korean Conflict.

My parents decided to make a big party because all their friends and family are united like old times.

Since my sister and me weren't baptized, they decided to have the Christening the same day. I was already 3 yrs. old and my sister 2 yrs. old.

Even though I was very young, I remember the church ceremony, the party and the guests. My sister doesn't remember anything.

What I remember very well about my christening were the outfits my grandmother Mama Lupe made.

The dresses were all lace. The shoes were satin and cute tiny sox. My sister and I looked just like two beautiful princesses from a fairy tale.

At Saint Conrado Church in Ponce Puerto Rico
CHRISTENING POEM

There were poems focusing on celebrating the baptism, the admittance of the newly baptized children, Adelin and Norma into the Christian family. It also conveyed congratulations to the parents and godparents.

There was also a poem said during the rituals ceremony.

At the end of the ceremony, there was a <u>Godparent Poem.</u>

This poem deals specifically with the relationship between godparents and godchildren. It also may be a message about the duty of godparents or the honor a godparent feeling for being asked to serve such a role.

All those words were said in Spanish… I heard that story from my mom.

<u>At the party</u>

What I remember about the party was the roasting of a pig. My father hired a couple of guys to do the roasting. My two grandmothers were too busy greeting the guests. My mom was busy with my sister and me.

My cousin, Luis Antonio, was in charge of making the ice cream. The good thing about this particular party was that the whole family was involved in putting everything together.

I recall my father chopping big blocks of ice for the soda, beer and juices. As he was getting ready to put the ice in huge iron buckets, he cut his hand. There was blood all over the place. He told my grandfather that it was just a scrape and kept working.

Chapter 10

Growing Up in Puerto Rico

As years went by, I was growing to be a very responsible young lady. I was always ready to help my siblings...

By the end of 1954, my family was expanding. I had two brothers and one sister. My mother needed help from her mother and the in-laws, but that wasn't enough.

Since I was the oldest, I had to work very hard to help my mother. Both of my grandmothers, Guadalupe and Ceferina taught me how to cook and clean. I even invented my own recipes with the help of my great-grandmother Mama Dolores.

By 1959, my parents had bought a larger house still close to my grandparents. We were rather happy...

I spend a lot of time playing with my sister Adelin. When Juan was learning how to walk, Julio was learning how to eat rice and beans.

I played a lot with other relatives. My aunts and uncles, on my father's side, were closed to my age. I was always laughing because my uncles tried to teach me boys stuff and my aunts were trying to teach me how to play with dolls.

I remember one time that my aunt Ana Dolores and I begged Mama Lupe to give us a chicken coop. There were a couple of them around the backyard. They kept lots of hens and roosters.

So, since my grandmother was always busy sewing or cooking, she wasn't really listening to my aunt and me. She told us to take any of them and to leave her work in peace.

We ran outside and started cleaning the place up. I swept while my aunt went inside the house to get small chairs and table that Papá Julio made for us. The furniture looked great.

We placed the cute little chairs with a table in a corner. My uncle Villen got rugs and Moncho started painting the outside of the tiny house. It was beginning to look like a real doll house. My other aunt Lucy was already living in New York, but we told her that we will take care of her dolls.

As soon as the doll house was finished, we all stepped out to admire our work. We all agreed that we made a master piece.

My uncle Kike didn't know about our project neither my father. They came home with some chickens and didn't tell anyone. It was getting dark, and my father took me home....

The following day, my sister and I got up very early. We were going to bring our favorite toys to the doll house. My mother gave us more pillows and dishes she didn't need.

When my sister and I went to my grandmother's house we got very angry. We found my aunt Ana Dolores crying. Moncho and Villen were also very upset. The chickens that my father and Kike brought the night before destroyed everything. There were bird drops all around the tiny house.

My grandmother had the nerves to scold us. She told us that we had no business making a doll house of a chicken cage. We reminded her that we got her permission to use anything we wanted in the backyard.

My grandmother apologized and asked my father and uncles to make us a real doll house. This time we even got our own blue prints for the house. It was beautiful. My grandfather cleaned the furniture and once again Villen and Moncho painted everything.

My aunt, my sister and I, made sandwiches and lemonade to celebrate the opening doors of our new doll house. It was really a job well done...

Life was going great for the Pagán family, however, Juan wanted more. He was in the National Guard and had a good job with the government. What he really wanted was to go abroad.

He kept talking about it and the whole family insisted that he didn't have to leave our beautiful island, Puerto Rico.

Chapter 11

The Visit September 1959

On one late autumn afternoon, we had a surprised visit from my mother's side of the family. It was her oldest brother, Pedro Morales Figueroa. He came for a short visit from New York. He was happy to see everyone.

When my uncle was about to go home, my father decided to talk to him. My uncle listened very carefully. He told my dad that it was a great idea to move to New York. My father was still in the National Guard and was a licensed plumber. He was prepared to work anywhere.

My parents didn't hesitate to make the big move. They thought about their four children. Since we were still very young, we wouldn't have any problem learning a second language. I have to admit that I was quite excited when I heard the good news.

All of us were asking plenty of questions. The best one was about the plane ride....

On September 9, 1959, my parents packed our bags and told us that my uncle Kike was going to drive one car and another family member another one....

During that time, there wasn't a highway. We had to take the old road all the way to the airport. The car that my uncle borrowed was a convertible. My uncle Villen, Moncho and Kike were happy to be with us until the last minute. It was a nice trip from Ponce to San Juan.

My uncle Kike just got his license, therefore, he was flying through those streets. We enjoyed the ride very much, but when we got to the airport, my parents and grandmother started yelling at my uncle Kike for speeding. He got scolded badly.

It was so sad saying goodbye to Mamá Lupe and the rest of the family. They stood at the gate until we were on the plane.

Once on the plane, my father was upset because the flight attendant wanted to put us on different sections of the plane. My dad told the young lady that we had tickets with seat numbers.

Each of us had our own seat. The reason for the misunderstanding was that the flight was overbooked. There were people with the same seat numbers. It took a while for us to get seated together, but we did it.

It was hard to sleep due to the movement of the plane. The old ladies took out their rosaries and started praying. At that point I was very scare. I thought that we were going to die.

Chapter 12

New York City

Puerto Rican culture in New York

Before I begin this chapter, I want to bring some history in my story because I believe it is important.

As soon as the Puerto Rican got to New York City, they began to form their own small "Barrios", in The Bronx, Brooklyn and in East Harlem, which would become known as Spanish Harlem.

It was in East Harlem where the Puerto Ricans established a cultural life of great vitality and sociality. Many participated in some of the sports, such as boxing and baseball.

This is interesting because those sports were first introduced in the island by the American Armed Forces right after the Spanish–American War.

Puerto Ricans who moved to New York took with them more than their customs and traditions. They took with them their famous "piraguas". A "piragua is a Puerto Rican frozen treat, shaped like a pyramid, made of shaved ice and covered with fruit flavored syrup.

According to Holding Aloft, the Banner of Ethiopia, by Winston James, "piraguas" were introduced in New York by Puerto Ricans as early as 1926.

Our talented Puerto Rican musicians and singers:

At "El Teatro Puerto Rico"......

Our Puerto Rican music flourished with the likes of Rafael Hernández and Pedro Flores who formed the "Trio Borincano". It gained recognition in New York City.

Let's not forget Myrta Silva who later joined Hernandez's "Cuarteto Victoria". She also gained fame as a singer after the group traveled and played throughout the United States.

The South Bronx became the main core for the Puerto Rican music. The theaters which had served to previous groups of immigrants, such as the Irish and the Italians, for their dramatic works or vaudeville style shows, now served the growing Puerto Rican and Latino population.

The musical performances from musicians from Puerto Rico and Latin America made a big difference in New York City. Families used to travel from all boroughs to the historical "Teatro Puerto Rico" located at E. 138th Street and Hunts Point in the Bronx.

The Teatro Puerto Rico's "golden era" lasted from 1947 to 1956. This is also the place where our dear musician José Feliciano made his stateside debut.

New York City became the center for freestyle music in the 1980s, of which Puerto Rican singer-songwriters represented a fundamental component.

Puerto Rican influence in popular music continues in the 21st century, surrounding major artists such as Jennifer Lopez.

The third great wave of domestic migration from Puerto Rico came after World War II. Nearly 40,000 Puerto Ricans settled in New York City in 1946 and 58,500 in 1952–53. Many soldiers who returned after World War II made use of the GI Bill and went to college.

For the Puerto Rican women, things were horrible in New York. They confronted economic exploitation, discrimination, racism, and the insecurities inherent in the migration process on a daily basis. Let me point out that even with the so many hardships, the women fared better than the men in the job market. The women left their homes for the factories in record numbers.

By 1953, Puerto Rican migration to New York reached its peak when 75,000 people left the island.......

Politics on the island and New York

In 1948, Puerto Ricans elected their first governor Luis Muñoz Marín, who together with his government initiated a series of social and economic reforms with the introduction of new programs in the island. Some of these programs met some resistance from the American government and therefore, the local government had some trouble implementing the same.

New York Mayor Robert F. Wagner, Jr. began a campaign to recruit Puerto Rican laborers in the island to work in the city's factories. Mayor Wagner figured that the city would benefit greatly by the luring of what was considered to be "cheap labor".

Discrimination was widespread in the United States and it was no different in New York. As stated by Lolita Lebron, there were signs in restaurants which read "No dogs or Puerto Ricans allowed".

The Puerto Rican Nationalist Party established an office in New York in 1950 and attracted many migrants. Leaders of the party conceived a plan that would involve an attack on the Blair House with the intention of assassinating United States President Harry S. Truman and also an attack on the House of Representatives.

These events had a negative impact on the Puerto Rican. Americans viewed Puerto Ricans as anti-Americans and the discrimination against them became even more widespread.

Many Puerto Ricans were able to overcome these obstacles and became respected members of their communities.

Among those respected member in the Puerto Rican community was Antonia Pantoja. She established organizations such as "ASPIRA" that helped many fellow countrymen to reach their goals.

The first New York Puerto Rican Day Parade was held on Sunday, April 12, 1958 in "El Barrio" located in Manhattan. Its first President was Victor Lopez and it was coordinated by José Caballero. The grand marshal was Oscar González Suarez.

There were many personalities from Puerto Rico present in that first parade. Even Luis Munoz Marin, the governor, was present.

The parade was organized to show Puerto Rican pride and its traditions. The parade still continues today in the city of New York. Let me tell you that it is also extended to other cities such as Chicago, Illinois and Orlando, Florida.

By 1960, the United States census showed that there were well over 600,000 New Yorkers of Puerto Rican birth or paternity. Estimates were that more than one million Puerto Ricans had migrated during that period.

Nuyorican Movement

The Nuyorican Poets Café......

Puerto Rican writer Jesús Colón founded an intellectual movement involving poets, writers, musicians and artists who are Puerto Rican or of Puerto Rican descent. They lived in or near New York City. Those people, which I admire, became known as the Nuyorican Movement. The phenomenon of the "Nuyoricans" came about when many Puerto Ricans who migrated to New York City faced difficult situations and hardships, such as racial discrimination.

Who is a "Nuyorican"? He or she is a simple Puerto Rican which developed a subculture.

In 1980, Puerto Rican poets Miguel Algarín, Miguel Piñero and Pedro Pietri established the "Nuyorican Poets Café". It is Located on Manhattan's Lower East Side 236 E 3rd Street, between Avenues B and C. This is now considered a New York landmark.

By 1964, the Puerto Rican community made up 9.3 percent of the total New York City's population. The Puerto Rican migrants who gained economic success began to move away from " El Barrios" and settled mostly in Westchester County or moved to other states.

At the present time, new immigrants from the Dominican Republic, Mexico and South America moved into the "Barrios". This area was once mainly occupied by the Puerto Ricans.

In the 1970s we saw what became known as reverse-migration. Many Puerto Ricans returned to the island to buy homes. Puerto Ricans returned to Puerto Rico to invest in local businesses.

I want to point out that Puerto Ricans have made many important contributions to New York and the society of the United States in general. They have contributed in the fields of entertainment, the arts, music, industry, science, politics, and the armed forces.

Since 2006, there has been recovery in migration from Puerto Rico to New York City and New Jersey. Apparently, multifactorial appealed to Puerto Ricans. It was primarily for economic and cultural considerations. The Census estimated for the New York City has increased from 723,621 in 2010, to 730,848 in 2012.

New York State overall has also resumed its net in-migration of Puerto Rican Americans since 2006. New York was the only state to register a decrease in its Puerto Rican population between 1990 and 2000. The Puerto Rican population of New York State still is the largest in the United States. It is estimated by the U.S. Census Bureau to have increased from 1,070,558 in 2010 to 1,103,067 in 2013.

New York State gained more Puerto Rican migrants from Puerto Rico as well as from elsewhere on the mainland between 2006 and 2012 than any other state in absolute numbers.

Also, unlike the initial pattern of migration several decades ago, this second Puerto Rican migration into New York is being driven by movement not only into New York City, but also into the city's surrounding suburban areas. New York City Metropolitan area gained the highest number of additional Puerto Rican Americans of any metropolitan area between 2010 and 2013.

As Puerto Ricans continue to climb the socioeconomic ladder and achieve a greater degree of professional occupations, the community is also purchasing homes in New Jersey's more affluent suburban towns.

Puerto Rican migration patterns, 1995-2000

Brooklyn has several neighborhoods with a Puerto Rican presence. Many of the ethnic Puerto Rican neighborhoods in Brooklyn were formed before the Puerto Rican neighborhoods in the South Bronx because of the work demand in the Brooklyn Navy Yard in the 1940s and 50s.

Bushwick has the highest concentration of Puerto Ricans in Brooklyn. Other neighborhoods with significant populations were Williamsburg, East New York, Brownsville, Coney Island, Red Hook, and Sunset Park.

In Williamsburg, Graham Avenue is nicknamed "Avenue of Puerto Rico" because of the high density and strong ethnic territory of Puerto Ricans who have been living in the neighborhood since the 1950s.

The Puerto Rican day parade is also hosted on the avenue....

Puerto Rican neighborhoods in Manhattan included Spanish Harlem and Loisaida. Spanish Harlem was "Italian Harlem" from the 1880s until the 1940s.

By 1940, however, the name "Spanish Harlem" was becoming widespread, and by 1950, the area was predominately Puerto Rican and African American.

Let's take a look at Loisaida

Loisaida is a district on the east of Avenue A. That district originally consisted of German, Jewish, Irish, and Italian working class residents. They lived in tenements without running water; the German presence, already in decline, virtually ended after the General Slocum disaster in 1904.

Since then, the community has become Puerto Rican and Latino in character, despite the "gentrification" that has affected the East Village and the Lower East Side since the late 20th century.

Staten Island has a fairly large Puerto Rican population along the North Shore, especially in the Mariners' Harbor, Arlington, Elm Park, Graniteville, Port Richmond and Stapleton neighborhoods, where the population is more or less 20%.

In New York and many other cities, Puerto Ricans usually live in close proximity with other Latinos and African Americans. There is also a large concentration of Puerto Ricans present in public housing developments throughout the city.

Puerto Ricans are present in large numbers throughout the Bronx. The Bronx has the highest percentage of Puerto Ricans of any borough. In some places in the South Bronx, Spanish is the primary language.

Throughout the 1970s, the South Bronx became known as the essence of a town weakening, but has since made a recovery.

Puerto Rican population in New York keeps increasing.......

As of 1990, New Yorkers of Puerto Rican descent, Nuyoricans, numbered 143,974. Nearly 41,800 state residents Nuyoricans in 1990 had lived in Puerto Rico in 1985.

According to the Census taken in the year 2000, Puerto Rican migrants make up a 1.2% of the total population of the United States with a population of well over 3 million Puerto Ricans including those of Puerto Rican descent.

You have to keep in mind that we are U.S. citizens. We shall never be excluded by the U.S. Census statistics of U.S. population. We make up about 2.5% of the total population of U.S. citizens around the world. I am talking about the inside and outside the U.S. mainland.

In July 1930, Puerto Rico's Department of Labor established an employment service in New York City....

The Migration Division known as the "Commonwealth Office", also part of Puerto Rico's Department of Labor, was created in 1948, and by the end of the 1950s, was operating in one hundred and fifteen cities.

The Department of Puerto Rican Affairs in the United States was established in 1989 as a cabinet-level department in Puerto Rico.

Currently, the Commonwealth operates the Puerto Rico Federal Affairs Administration, which is headquartered in Washington, D.C. and has twelve regional offices throughout the United States.

Puerto Ricans in New York have preserved their cultural heritage by being involved actively in the different political and social rights movements in the United States. They founded "Aspira", a leader in the field of education, in 1961.

When I was in high school, I used to work in an afternoon program funded by Aspira. My job was to teach writing skills to Puerto Ricans young adults. It helped many teenagers score high in the S.A.T's.

Let me tell you that Aspira still is one of the largest national Latino nonprofit organizations in the United States.

There are other educational and social organizations founded by Puerto Ricans in New York. I am proud to say that I worked in the National Puerto Rican Forum from 1985 thru 1994. I started as an English Instructor. I was promoted to Head Instructor in 1986.

The reason I left that wonderful institution was that I was offered a job as an English teacher in the public school system.

Now let me return to my relocation to New York.... September 10, 1959......

We got to New York City at about 4:00 a.m. yet, it was very dark and so ugly. When we got off the plane, I started to cry. Adelin and the boys kept their mouth shut. They really had no idea of the whole situation. They were just confused.

That autumn day on September 10, 1959 was the very same day that the Department of Sanitation in New York was on strike. There was garbage everywhere. The smell was nasty that I started thinking about Puerto Rico.

I had flashbacks of my room full of stuffed animals and the books my grandfather gave me. I just cried in silence because I didn't want my parents to know how sad I was. I left behind more than material things. I left behind the so many people that really loved me. My grandfather, Julio, didn't say goodbye. He didn't know that he wouldn't see us ever again.

My parents had other problems. We really didn't have a place to live. It wasn't easy finding a five room apartment.

My dear uncle Pedro Morales and his family tried very hard to help. They told my parents not to worry. My uncle had a plan. He informed my mother that there was one solution. The plan was to separate the family.

We had to live with different family members. My sister and I stayed with my uncle Pedro and the boys went to live with my parents in another part of Brooklyn with my uncle Ruben.

You know I really enjoyed living with my cousins in the projects. We were one big happy family.

My father had an education, a good job and earned enough money to raise a family in Puerto Rico, therefore, he had no problem in New York. It didn't take long for him to find a job and at the same time an apartment.

Still, I wasn't happy. In school, I told my sister not to speak English. My plan was to stay quiet so that we can be sent to Puerto Rico.

One morning, while in school, my cousin was sent to my classroom to translate something, because my teacher couldn't get any information from me.

When my 4th grade teacher, Mrs. Kramer spoke to my cousin, I started to laugh. I began speaking in English. The teacher was surprised, because I expressed myself very well.

Chapter 13

Do you believe in Angels?

It was a cool Autumn day when I saw a little girl all by herself in the school yard. She was very sad. There were many students playing, however, everyone just passed by her and never stopped to ask her why she was there alone.

She was dressed in a worn black coat, broken shoes and very dirty. This girl just sat and watched the children play.

She never spoke to anyone. Many students were playing ball around her. Sometimes they would bump into her, but they kept on with their game.

The following day, I decided to go to the school yard before entering the school. I was very curious about that little girl because I didn't see her inside the school the previous day.

I walked very fast towards the school yard. I didn't want my teacher or classmates to see me. I was very surprised to see the little girl in the same spot as the day before.

As I was walking, I thought to myself that this it isn't a place for a young child. I was in the 6th grade almost 11 years old. The young kids were supposed to be in the school yard with their teachers and some parents.

When I got closer, I could see the back of the her dress. It was disturbingly shaped. I figured that was the reason the other kids just passed by and made no effort to speak to her.

Deformities are a low blow to our society and heaven forbid if you take a step to help someone who is different.

The little girl lowered her eyes slightly when I approached her. I got so close to her by this time that I could see her shape. She was badly deformed.

I smiled to let her know it was OK; I was there to help, to talk. I sat down beside her and opened with a simple, "Hello"; the little girl acted in shocked and mumbled a "hi"; after a long stare.

I smiled and she shyly smiled back. We talked until it was time to go to class. The school yard was completely empty. I asked her why she was so sad.

She looked at me with a sad face said, "Because I'm different"; I immediately I said, "That you are!" and smiled. The little girl acted even sadder. Then I and said, "I know." "You remind me of an angel, sweet and innocent."

She looked at me and then slowly got to her feet and said, "Really?" "Yes, you're like a little Guardian Angel sent to watch over me" She reply in a sweet tone of voice, yes, and smiled.

With that she opened the back of her black coat and allowed her wings to spread. She then said "I am. I'm your Guardian Angel," It was a beautiful sight to see her with a twinkle in her eyes.

I was speechless -- sure I was seeing things." She said, "For once you thought of someone other than yourself. My job here is done;" I got to my feet and said, "how come no one stopped to talk to you?" She looked at me, and said, "You were the only one that could see me," and then she was gone.

After that incident in the school yard, I started to feel so different. I began to change the minute I walked into my classroom. I didn't know if I was going crazy or not, but I could tell you one thing, I went to class so sure about myself.

You see, it was testing day. I was given a very hard examination. I just moved from Puerto Rico. According to everyone, I wasn't smart enough because I didn't speak any English.

A couple of weeks passed by. The test results indicated that I had a very high score. I passed test in flying colors. I proved to my teacher that I was very intelligent.

My parents were informed that I would finish the semester, and that in January 1960, I would be transferred to Public School 169. The education in that school was much better. I proved to everyone that my IQ was better than any other kid in my class.

As months turned into years, my brothers and sister also were transferred to Public School 169. The four of us were placed in honor classes.

In those days there were no English as a Second Language taught in any public school in New York. The mainstream teachers used the swim or sink method.

That meant that if you didn't learn English on your own, you would fail in class and in the business world.

When we were at home, we spoke Spanish; however, the minute we were in the streets, English came naturally.

Sometimes I think about my guardian angel and wonder if the whole thing was real or not. My sister was the only one that knew that story. We used to talk about it, but as years went by, we were too busy to even sit together and remember our bad times at Public School 27.

Things were getting better for my parents by the mid 60's. My father found a better job as a plumber which paid well. He made so much money that within a couple of years, we moved to a bigger house with a backyard.

My siblings got used to the idea of living in New York. I wasn't happy. That was the reason I didn't speak in class. I thought that if I stayed mute, I would be sent to my beautiful island, Puerto Rico.

Sometimes, when I am sad, memories of my guardian angel come to mind. Not many people have gone through that experience. I guess I was blessed because when I think of something negative, I smile as I remember that cute little girl that helped me with my self-esteem when I was young.

Chapter 14

First Christmas in New York

Children have much vivid imagination to forget about bad experiences at home or in school....

The following chapter will indicate how I managed to forget about my environment by just imagining things...

I was only ten when I first saw him. I remember that switch from one situation around my surrounding to the other. I used to have imaginary friends and it worked fine for a while.....

I used to make believe that I will get help from God. Why did I think like that? Well, to begin with, when I had an assignment, I did it with no problem.

I remember on particular day so clearly. It was right after school started on September 1959, my first week in school in New York.....

Many people came to see the apartment on the second floor, but they said that it was too small for their family.

On that autumn day of 1959, I just knew that the man that took the apartment was going to be my friend. He wasn't too tall and his hair was white and long.

He also had a close-cropped white beard. By the way, the lady next door smiled when she saw him. I guessed he must have reminded her of someone from yesteryears. He was carrying a box; it was marked "early birds" on its side.

There were some moving men helping him. He kept very busy all day long. Some neighbors wanted to know what he did for a living, but no one even dared to ask him.

Two weeks went by and as it did, I watched the new tenant very closely. I'd hear him in his apartment listening to music, TV, and talking. I never got close enough to actually hear what was said in his living room, but we shared a wall between our kitchens.

One day, mom caught my sister and me with a glass against my ear. I put the glass very close on the wall trying to hear the conversation next door. Boy; did we get into trouble for that!

We were grounded for three days. That was the punishment for ease-dropping, as mom called it. Adelin didn't want to play detective with me. She didn't want any part of my game. My brothers were too small to know about the game.

So, I was on my own....

The next day, I ran into my new neighbor after my three days of punishment. He was coming in as I was going out. I was hurrying and just as I jumped from the second step of the stairs, he came in the front door and we crashed together. He fell backwards but as he did, he caught me and saved me from falling.

The door slammed into his back and I heard him grunt from it hitting him. I just knew I'd be in more trouble, so as soon as he let me go, I started apologizing like crazy.

He stood there for a minute, then raised his hand chuckling. I thought he was going to hit me! Instead, he said, whoa, slow down young lady... it's not a problem. I would have done the same thing if I were your age.

Then... he started laughing. "In fact" he said, "I have done it in my younger days". I asked him, are you going to tell on me? My mom will kill me if you do. He smiled and said, No, it's our secret, you don't tell, I won't tell.

He told me that his name was Mr. Reilly. I found it strange that he didn't tell me his first name. It didn't matter. I always use last names with people not related to me….

After a couple of days, Mr. Reilly offered me a job; he paid me to take out his trash. He would sit it outside his door every other morning, and I would take it on my way out to school.

He paid me five dollars a week. My parents thought it was too much but he insisted. I thought to myself that Mr. Reilly was a cool guy.

He was a little over weight and older than my parents……

I was so curious about Mr. Reilly. He always had some visitors, which I never saw coming or leaving. Some of them only stayed for maybe an hour. I was just guessing. This Mr. Nice Guy may be a spy.

I was also very puzzled by the end of October because I didn't know what Mr. Reilly did as far as work. I began to guess again. He was maybe a secret agent or something. He didn't work hours like my father or Mr. Alvarez in apartment 2B.

I noticed he was home when I got home from school and he was there when I left in the morning. Sometimes he was gone for two or three days, but he still paid me the five dollars even if I only took his trash out once that week.

One day, I overheard him talking to someone inside his place. It appeared he was upset about something. I heard the other man say that it wasn't his fault.

He also stated that it would be ready on time. I could tell he was nervous, and then they came out. They stopped in the hall in front of Mr. Reilly apartment. They closed the door as they left. I heard Mr. Reilly say something about being disappointed, and they left the building.

I tried to figure out what the whole deal meant, but it was over my head. The visitor was small like me. I think they call people like that midgets. He was dressed funny, in clothes no one wore in my neighborhood.

After that incident, I started pretending I was a secret agent, and it was my job to spy on the other spies especially the one who lived next door.

Things went back to normal after Mr. Reilly settled down. Since he didn't visit anyone that lived in our building, it was kind of boring spying on him. I knew better than to try listening again through the wall. If I got caught again by my mom, I would be grounded forever.

One afternoon, it dawned on me that I have never seen the inside Mr. Reilly's apartment. I told my sister to take a walk with me. Adelin, so shy said, "No. I don't want to get in trouble." She claimed that Christmas was around the corner and she wanted nice presents.

I still was determined to see Mr. Reilly's apartment. I thought I would ask him to help me with my homework. I went to his door, and as I was about to knock, I heard, come-in young lady, it's open. I don't know how he knew that it was me, but I did as he said.

As I walked in, he was sitting at a desk. I noticed it was only one of three pieces of furniture in the room. He had a TV, a couch, a desk and a chair.

On the desk there were letters, lots, and lots of letters. I couldn't see who they were from. Mr. Reilly had gotten up from the desk and met me before I could get close enough to see. He smiled at me and said, "So; you need help with your homework do you?"

Surprised, I asked... how do you know? He again smiled; his eyes seem to sparkle as he did. It made me feel like everything was okay; it made me forget he knew beforehand.

Why aren't you out riding your bike he asked? I don't have a bike, I answered. The next thing I knew, and I was leaving his apartment with my homework and completed.

When I returned to my apartment, I looked at the clock over the TV; one and a half hours had passed, and all I remembered was we had done my homework. That's when I knew Mr. Reilly was someone special.

In mid-November, there was a big argument between Mr. and Mrs. Rentas up in apartment 3A. It started out kind of easy with only one word.

Then it got louder until finally everyone in the building heard it. My parents told me I wasn't allowed to go upstairs. I wanted to go and see them fight, but my mother said if I put one foot on those stairs, I would be grounded for a month. So, I just stood at the stairway and listened.

Then, everything got very quiet and I heard…"It isn't nice to find pleasure in another's misery." I turned around and looking at me with the happiest smile was Mr. Reilly. He said; " excuse me," and then he stepped passed me and went upstairs.

A few minutes later, I heard a door close. Then, Mr. Reilly came down smiling more than before. He went to his apartment not saying a word.

Mr. and Mrs. Rentas had stopped fighting. There was no yelling or fighting. All that I could hear was the normal sounds of pipes rattling, people walking, and other normal sounds of a three story brick apartment building.

Two days before Thanksgiving, my parents sent Adelin and me went to Mr. Reilly's apartment. They wanted to invite him to our Thanksgiving's dinner. They said they didn't know if he had plans. My parents thought that it would be nice to have him. It would also be the neighborly thing to do.

So, we went next door…

We knocked and stood waiting for him to say come in. We waited and a few minutes went by and we knocked again. Still there was no answer.

We decided to try the door and to my surprise it was unlocked. As we pushed it open, we said," Mr.. Reilly? Are you here?" When he didn't answer, we opened the door more and stepped inside.

By this time, Adelin was so scared that she just wanted to leave. I told her that I have to look around. As I did, I noticed everything seemed the same from the last time I was there. The only difference was that there weren't any letters on the desk. Adelin couldn't take it anymore and left me alone....

I was concentrating on my investigation. I saw now that there is a roll of paper with names laying there. I was just about to reach for it when I heard, "It's not polite to invite ones self-inside another's home!" I jumped about two feet then turned around. There, smiling as always was Mr. Reilly, eyes twinkling.

Well young lady; "Do you have a message for me?" I just stood there, embarrassed. "Well?" He said. I stared at him a moment then I remembered why I had gone to his apartment; oh yeah, I started talking.

My parents wanted me to invite you to our house for Thanksgiving's dinner. Mr. Reilly's smile widened and he replied; tell your parents that I would be happy to join your family on that special holiday. He also asked me if he needed to bring anything. It was my turn to smile; only your appetite I replied.

Thanksgiving Day

Mom brushed off her apron as she went to answer the door. I was busy mashing potatoes and my sister was setting the table when we heard the knock. "Am I too early?" I heard Mr. Reilly say after Mom opened the door. "Goodness No!" You're just in time, my father replied with joy. The boys were playing and I was finishing mashing potatoes.

As I walked into the living room, I felt very happy. My brothers and my parents were talking to Mr. Reilly. Then Mr. Reilly said, "Oh... I almost forgot" Mr. Reilly handed dad a paper bag with something inside.

My father pulled out what looked like a bottle of wine, and stated; Now Mr. Reilly, you didn't have to do this. I guess I kind of frowned because Mr. Reilly smiled at me and said to my father, it isn't wine, its Sparkling cider, these young children are too young to drink.

Also, I don't indulge myself. We walked to the table where Mom asked my sister and me to help bring the remaining items from the kitchen. The boys were happy to sit next to Mr. Reilly.

My father sat at the head of the table and my mom beside him. My sister and I were sitting side by side. Our Thanksgiving dinner wasn't anything special; Mom had baked a small turkey which she bought on special. We had mashed potatoes, rice, peagent peas, green salad, stuffing and cranberry sauce. . For dessert Mom had made a flan topped with cool whip.

After dinner, Mr. Reilly helped clean up and then he offered to wash the dishes. My first thought was alright! No dishes for me tonight, but as usual, I was wrong.

Mom told Mr. Reilly guest don't do dishes in our home, "do they my dear daughter?" Knowing what was next; I said no, and I went to the kitchen with Adelin and started the water. My parents and Mr. Reilly talked for a while then I heard him say, you must let me supply Christmas dinner and with that he left.

December came and with it, all the songs, commercials, and billboards. My dad was working two jobs by now. The money was just to pay the rent and bills.

My parents had enough money to get us a present and a tree. I already knew we wouldn't have much, but we were used to it. Christmas was never my favorite time of the year because I saw how it bothered my parents. They didn't feel comfortable in New York as they did in Puerto Rico. Money was very tight.

During the next few days, I saw Mr. Reilly often. He was either coming or going to his apartment. On the first Friday of the month, he had pinned an envelope to his trash, it just said "READ THIS". Inside was a note that read, I'm sure you'll need this before Christmas, consider it an advance pay for the month. Attached was a twenty dollar bill. The note was written in red ink. After that I rarely saw Mr. Reilly.

I saw the midgets several times during the next two weeks, but Mr. Reilly only once.

A couple of days before Christmas, Mr. Reilly was on his way out, with a big suit bag like those used when traveling. I asked him what was in it, he looked at me and with a sly smile, replied, "Why, my Santa suit of course!" Then he started chuckling.

I just thought he was being a wise guy and smiled back. He continued walking down the hall humming jingle bells as he did.

Two days before Christmas, I saw Mr. and Mrs. Rentas carrying groceries into the building. They never looked happier. Mrs. Rentas whispered softly to her husband as they walked.

All the neighbors heard Mrs. Rentas told them that her husband had stopped drinking. He was even working and helping around the house.

On Christmas Eve, my father sent me to ask Mr. Reilly if he wanted to join us for some "coquito" and "arroz con dulce".

I knocked and knocked, but he didn't answer. I put my ear to the door and listened, but heard nothing. I went back and told my parents that he wasn't home.

When I returned to our apartment, Mr. and Mrs. Rentas stopped by, then, Mr. Rodriguez and the Smith family showed up.

Next thing we knew, there were several people at our tiny apartment talking, and drinking "coquito". Mr. Rodriguez took out a guitar and started playing "parranda" songs, slowly, everybody started singing.

I couldn't help but wish Mr. Reilly was here too. It was almost midnight when everyone left. My parents and I picked up the glasses and took them to the kitchen.

Mom told us to leave everything in the sink. All the dishes will be cleaned in the morning. I filled the sink with dish washing detergent. I placed the glasses and small dishes in the sink. I went back into the living room with my father.

Adelin and the boys have been sleeping for a couple of hours by now. They went to sleep early so that Christmas morning would get here faster.

Our tree was only about two feet tall, but it was beautiful. We all helped with the decoration. My father let each one of us put the tinsel and decoration while he did the lights.

We stood still, in the living room looking at the tree; there were only seven presents under it. Each of us had one gift from my parents.

I got one for Mr. Reilly. I looked up at my parents and they were smiling at me. They knew that I was thinking about Puerto Rico, but still, love filled the room...

On Christmas morning, I woke up hearing my parent's saying "Oh my goodness!" I quickly rushed into the living room and couldn't believe my eyes. The tree we had only the night before had grown. It was an easy six feet tall, fully decorated and sparkling like it was covered with stars. Underneath it there were presents lots and lots of presents.

In the dining room, the table was filled with food, ham, turkey and dressing. There were all kinds of food. Even Christmas cookies. My parents were amazed. Where did it all come from they whispered.

We looked at each other and, at the same time said, "What happened?" I started to reach for one of the many gifts when I saw a note tied to a branch of the tree.

I pulled it off and looked at it; all that was written on it was, "To the Pagán family". I handed it to Mom and waited as she opened it. I watched as she silently read the note inside.

Tears welled up in her eyes and started rolling down her face. Mom, what is it I asked. She looked at me and smiled, she handed me the note and I read, Merry Christmas. It was signed with S. Nicholas. Who is this person? I asked.

My Parents smiled again and said, the answer is found with the gifts. Each gift was signed your friend, S. Nicholas.

Who is S. Nicholas I again asked? My father reached down, picked up a gift wrapped in shiny red wrapping paper, here, he said, to my sister and maybe this one will answer your question.

There wasn't a name tag on it. She quickly ripped it open, and inside she found Barbie doll. Adelin longed for that doll for years. In the box was a note, it said, "It isn't polite to question a gift origins", Love; Mr. Reilly. You may know me better as Saint Nicholas or Santa for short.

That was one great Christmas morning, even though we were far away from Puerto Rico.

This story, my friends, was just a dream...

Chapter 15

New Year 1960

January 1960, Adelin and I were ready for Public School 169…

You know, I found out that not only the education was better at our new school, but also the teachers.

We made friends right away. I became class president and tutor to some of my class mates.

So many years have gone by and I still think of my precious island.

My grandfather, Julio Pagan Torres died on October 10, 1964 and my great-grandmother in June 1972. Guadalupe was left alone. She sold her house, in Ponce, and moved to New York. I was a bit happy because I can be with all my uncles and aunts.

My grandmother Guadalupe taught me more stuff. I learned how to sew my own clothing and my cooking was superb!

I graduated from Prospect Heights High School and was accepted at Colombia University.

I was also qualified to work in the New York City Police Department. I was happy because I have accomplished a lot.

While in the Police Department, I met what I thought was the love of my life, a Police Officer. He was really a "Latin Lover". He didn't speak Spanish at all. I made so much fun of him.

As we started dating, he didn't like the idea of having a chaperone. He was born in New York and his upbringing was different from mine.

He had so many girlfriends that I guessed he only came to visit me because he liked my cooking. Our little romance lasted only a few months because I informed him that I wasn't part of his dolls' collection. I wished him well and that was the end of it.

I kept working in the Police Department and I also kept studying.

The minute I graduated from the University, I knew was ready for a vacation. I couldn't believe that after almost twenty years I was finally going to my island.

My mother started making plans. She wanted to see her family and this was a good chance to do so. My sister and my friend Beverly also wanted to go with me. I was happy to return to Puerto Rico with my sister and mom. I couldn't sleep all night. I just wanted to be on that plane to see a few cousins and my grandmother Ceferina Figueroa Bello.

Chapter 16

Returning to Puerto Rico 1972

The flight was great. We were greeted at the airport by some of my relatives. My uncle Kike, as always, was waiting for us. He didn't want to miss the opportunity of seeing my first reaction as we were heading towards Ponce.

Everything was so different. Now there is a highway. The trip to the south part of Puerto Rico is more enjoyable. The scenery is awesome. My cousins kept asking us about the rest of the family in New York. We just kept talking and told them many events that had happened to each family member.

We got to Ponce about 1 p.m. without a problem.

Our first hour was spent unpacking a handing out gifts. It was great seeing my cousins on the Pagán side of the family.

Kike was the only one that didn't relocate to New York. He had a good job in P.R. He and his wife Migdalia were happy raising their three children. Life for them was great on the island.

The following day we got up early and went to see my grandmother Ceferina. My mother was anxious to see Mamá Nina. She was living with my Aunt Emma and her family.

When we got to "Jardines Del Caribe", Lourdes and her two brothers were waiting for us. Right away they told us that we were going dancing that night. The dance was going to take place at the university which they were attending.

I informed them that I wanted to meet a guy from the university. I also stated that he should have the same interests as me.

My aunt was quite happy to see us. She made a great feast on our behalf. My grandmother Ceferina was all smiles when she saw all of us sitting in the dining room.

After eating a big lunch, we started making plans for the evening. I told my cousin Angel that I was ready for that great dance. He laughed when I reminded him that I was searching for a husband.

When we got to the dance, it was hard to get a table. The place was packed. The music was blasting. I didn't mind having a table because I went there to dance. I never sit during a dance or party.

At the dance

I danced with a lot of my cousin's' friends. They were very polite. These guys were so different from the ones I met in New York City.

When the dance was almost over, I asked my cousin about the young man I was going to meet. My cousin laughed. He was here; however, he saw you dancing and left without saying a word.

We got to my aunt's house about 2 a.m. My mother and aunt were up. They wanted to hear about our adventure. They both enjoyed listening to us. We told them that we really had a great time. As always, Tía Emma made sandwiches and coffee. We ate and went to sleep.

The following day, we all got up at about 11 a.m. I was well rested. I was walking around in my pajamas when my cousin informed that the so call mystery young man was coming to meet me during lunch.

I just looked at Angel and told him to forget it. I wasn't planning on going out or fixing myself up for some fool that didn't bother to talk to me during the dance. My cousin told me that it was too late. The young man was parking his car in front of the house.

Well, too late to get dress to impress a fool. I sat with my hair in curlers. I had no makeup on and still with my pajamas. I was too busy eating an "asopao de pollo" that my aunt made. I didn't even look up to see this guy.

He pulled a chair and sat across from me. He introduced himself. My name is Eliezer Ramos, your future husband. I started laughing so hard that I chocked. He also said that I looked good with no makeup and wearing my pajamas. I believe it was a funny sight.

I was very impressed by this young man. He spoke English with no accent whatsoever. He told me that he was a senior at the Catholic University of Ponce. He wanted to be a doctor. He also told me about his hobbies and that he enjoyed the beach and all water sports.

We spoke for a couple of hours. I even forgot that it wast 3 p.m. I was still with my pajamas talking to a total stranger. I excused myself took a shower and got dressed.

I put on a pair of white shorts, blue short sleeves blouse. I wore a nice pair of sandals. My hair was very long so I just made a pony tail. I wasn't ready to impress this guy that saw me earlier in my pjs…

As I walked into the living room, he just kept looking at me. I asked him what was wrong with my outfit. He said I looked gorgeous. I just smile.

He informed me that we were going out that night. I reminded him that it doesn't work like that. He was supposed to ask me first and if I agreed, we would go out that night.

He apologized and asked me if I would like to go for a drive and perhaps a movie. I told him sure, but that my cousins were going with me. He said that he was expecting that.

Before we were off to the movies, he told me that he wanted me to meet two of his friends. My cousin Lourdes was smiling when we reached a house located a couple of blocks from my family.

I got out of the car and found it very strange that no one greeted us. He went into the house as if he was the owner. He told us to sit in the living room and we did. I looked at my cousin Lourdes because she still had that grin I didn't like.

Suddenly, my mystery man walked into the living room with an elderly couple. I was very puzzled. He said to them, "Papí, Mamí, esta es mi novia Norma".

I was in a state of shock. This fool introduced me to his parents as his girlfriend. They both smiled and were very pleased to meet me. Then an older sister, Delia, also came out to meet me. She was so happy because her younger brother had a girlfriend.

Delia asked him what our plans were for the evening. He told her about the drive in movie and then sightseeing around Ponce.

Delia didn't hesitate in giving her brother her car keys. Her car was a super beetle. It was brand new!

The movie was great... it was Love Story...

After the movie, we went for some ice-cream and for a walk around "la Plaza"....

The next day, he came for breakfast. My cousin invited him without telling me. I was already used to the idea of everyone trying to hook me up with this guy. As the day before, he saw me in my pjs...

We ate breakfast; however, this time even my grandma, Ceferina, joined us. I guessed she was also in this matching adventure.

Time was going very fast..... I was getting so used to the idea of seeing this guy. I had to return to New York. I was counting the days, the hours and minutes. I have to leave my island once again....

As we were heading towards the airport, Eliezer held my hand and said, "I am going to New York and we are going to get marry". I have to admit, I didn't want to leave him. I don't know if I was used to him or that I really cared for him.

The whole family took us to the airport.

When I got to New York, I was a complete different person. My parents asked me what was wrong with me. I told them that I miss Puerto Rico. I didn't go into details about meeting my future husband.

Eliezer was calling me at least three times a week. I wrote to him. Communication in 1972 wasn't that easy. The calls were expensive.

On September 1972, Eliezer told me that he was moving to New York. He was going to stay with his brother Eliot.

The minute Eliezer arrived; he made arrangement to go for a job interview. My sister Adelin helped him with the application. He was applying for a job with the U.S. Government, Food and Drugs Administration.

Adelin introduced Eliezer to the head of that department. He took the test and within weeks he was working for FDA as an Inspector.

Things were going well that in February 17, 1973, we got married. It was a beautiful wedding. The bride's mates were dressed in 18th century outfits. Those dresses were beautiful. All the girls' dresses were in burgundy, but my sister's and Ida.

Their dresses were pink. They each had a parasol made of flowers. We all had the same hairdo long banana curls. The ushers wore long tail tux. It was a wedding straight from a fairy tale. It was also full of love.

The church was well decorated with white flowers.

My flower girl was my cousin Ada. She was only 6 yrs. old and the ring bearer was Kermit, Eliezer's nephew.

After the church ceremony, we went to the reception hall. It was a very lovely place in Brooklyn. The food was excellent. We had a choice of chicken or roast beef, vegetables etc. The cake was three levels and very beautiful. My grandmother made the favors and center pieces. She also made my wedding dress. Thanks to Mama Lupe it was truly a beautiful reception.

We went to the Poconos at Mount Airy Lodge, Pennsylvania for our honeymoon. It was below zero, therefore, we had all the winter sports which we enjoy practicing. We were there for one week.

When we got home, Adelin had already counted the money we received as wedding gifts. With all that money, we bought our first car.

My father was very happy because he had time to finish an apartment that he was going to rent. He told us to stay there until we had enough money to buy a house. We lived there rent free. Within a couple of months, we bought a house.

Moving day.....

We found our dream house in Ozone Park, Queens NY. It was a corner house. I felt in love with it the minute I saw it. My father, brothers and friends did the moving.

We started decorating and buying furniture. Things were going great.

Eliezer was a loving husband. He was always trying to please me. We kept studying.....

Days turned into weeks and then into years. We have been married for almost 5 years when we decided to have a child....

I got pregnant, but had a miscarriage. I was very sad...

On that same year that I had the miscarriage, I told Eliezer that it was time to move to Puerto Rico. I wanted to return to my island. He made the necessary arrangement and his supervisor transferred him to San Juan. I was happy once again.

We bought a house in Bayamon. It had four bedrooms, two bathrooms, living room, dining room and a big kitchen. The backyard and garage were nice. I had a place to do my gardening. Life once again was great.

One Sunday afternoon, when we were visiting his parents, the baby topic came up. We didn't tell his family the reason I lost the baby...

Eliezer still wanted to make me happy in every possible way. I told him that I felt comfortable just being in Puerto Rico with his family and my parents.

I was in love with my husband. I didn't care if I had a child or not, however, on June 30, 1985, we were divorced.

My sister in-law Delia died just a couple of weeks before we moved to Puerto Rico. I was very sick for a while. Delia was a sweetheart. She left two children a baby boy of 4 yrs. and a girl of only 6 months. Delia had a brain tumor and died at a very young age.

I know that if Delia would have been alive today, Eliezer and I would have survived every obstacle in life.

I am sorry to say that Micaela Ramos and Adolfo Ramos, Eliezer's parents, died many years after our divorce. I will never forget them…

I still keep in touch with some of Eliezer's nieces and nephews. The Ramos family was part of me and will always be…..

After the divorce, in 1985, I returned to New York. I had plenty of friends which helped me get a good job teaching at the Puerto Rico National Forum. I got a beautiful apartment, bought a nice car and did well for myself.

After a couple of years at the Forum, I resigned. I took the National Teaching Examination and was certified to teach in the City of New York. The benefits were better. I loved working with children and young adults.

I also helped people living with aids. Counseling young adults about this sickness wasn't easy.

In 1994, I started working as an instructor/counselor for Housing Works. This is an organization located in Broadway and Houston in New York City.

It has now lots of other offices throughout the City of New York. It was great helping my clients. Some came out of jail with nothing and were very grateful in receiving a helping hand.

For the homeless and people with Aids, this organization is heaven…

On cold weekends I always volunteered to work in soup kitchens. I used to get a couple of chickens, rice, vegetable and plenty of beans from the Hispanic store owners. They didn't hesitate in giving us supply of any kind because it was for a good cause.

The homeless were always waiting for their meals in front of the soup kitchen; however, when they saw me it was different. They knew they were going to get the best lunch ever.

I enjoyed seeing them happy. Sometimes I gave them clothes and blankets. My job was really to help them get into the program at Housing Works.

Even though I was working for the Job Training Department, I went as a volunteer in the library that was in the making. Housing Works

Inc. receives hundreds of educational materials daily. I enjoyed classifying books and getting them ready for sale.

The good thing about the library was the way it was arranged. It was also a coffee shop; therefore we named it Housing Works Book Store Café.

I was happy, but still I wanted to move to Puerto Rico. I was tired of the cold weather. My parents weren't doing well. My mom was sick all the time and my dad with diabetes and chronic arthritis.

Many years went by and I still had the desire to live in my island....

On January 16, 1997, I went to Puerto Rico for a visit. My dad, who had relocated to the island back in 1980, was working for the Puerto Rico National Guard. He asked me if I wanted to work there. Right away I replied...yes!

I returned to New York and got all my documentation ready for Puerto Rico. I had a secondary teaching license and had plenty of experience. I was fully qualified for my job as an English Instructor to a second to none organization.

I moved to Puerto Rico and even with all my qualifications, I had to work for Puerto Rico board of education for at least one year. I worked as an English Teacher at "el Colegio Ponceño" for one year and then in the public school system for six months. It wasn't easy. The kids in both schools were very poor in English. They had no respect for teachers.

I had a big problem, my Spanish was horrible. I spoke to them only in English. I informed their parents, in both schools, that speaking to their kids in English was the only way they would learn.

The directors and parents agreed with me, however, the students didn't. They told me that their previous teachers used to teach them songs. They would sing all day and had a practice test before any big examination. My method was no singing. They were already in the 9th thru 12th grade. Singing days were over. Their reading comprehension and writing skills were the pits.

Guess what? I survived both private and public schools in Puerto Rico. I got my elementary and secondary teaching licenses. I was ready for the National Guard.

When I told my students at "La Ferran" Public school that I was leaving, they started to cry. They liked my method of teaching. I even paid for their graduation hall because that sector is very poor. I also was in the refreshment committee for the graduating class. I informed them not to worry. I was going to leave the money with the president of the committee.

Also, I told them that I was going to be present on graduation day. The graduation class gave me a medal and also a gigantic postcard signed by all my students. It was a very emotional day… I was sad but at the same time happy because some of my ex- students were going to join the National Guard and I was going to be their English Instructor once again.

Chapter 17

January 1999

The Language Center, Fort Allen Juana Diaz PR

Before I begin writing about my work at the Language Center, I will narrate a few facts of this wonderful institution.

The Puerto Rico National Guard Language Center was established in 1976. It has performed its mission of providing English language training to Non-prior service Warriors, Airmen, military families, and Puerto Rico National Guard citizen Warriors.

It was originally founded as the English Technical Language School. This school was located at Camp Santiago Training Site in Salinas, Puerto Rico. It has been functioning as a State-operated educational program within the Puerto Rico Army National Guard for over 40 yrs.

It aimed at reducing the number of trainees returning from Basic Training. The problem was that if the new applicants didn't go to the Language Center, they would be returning from the United States due to lack of proficiency in the English language.

The Defense Language Institute English Language Center at Lackland, Air Force Base, in Texas approved the Puerto Rico National Guard Language Center as a non-resident English Language Training Program in 1979.

It wasn't until 1984 that the National Guard Bureau approved federal funding to operate the Language Center.

The following year, in May 1985, the Language Center relocated to its present site at Fort Allen, Juana Diaz, and PR.

The Language Center has a very important vision. The vision is that it has to be an accredited, prestigious institution. The school would facilitate language acquisition and military skills.

I know it can be done because all instructors are fully qualified. It is also aiming in the transformation, readiness and retention of Warriors and Airmen for America's Army and Joint Forces.

The PUERTO RICO NATIONAL GUARD LANGUAGE CENTER conducts an intensive full-time ENGLISH LANGUAGE TRAINING program consisting of seven hours daily of English instruction, five days a week.

In addition, students are normally assigned two hours of homework/study hall daily. The AMERI-CAN LANGUAGE COURSE curriculum consists of a combination of classroom learning and individual language laboratory instruction. They also receive military classes.

The students don't go home on weekends; therefore, they are speaking English 24/7. Family members are allowed to come for visits on Sunday afternoons. During some holidays, students pack their belonging and head home.

When I began teaching at the Language Center, what I like best was the discipline. Every day I looked forward on going into a classroom where students are there to learn.

All instructors at the Language Center are well qualified. They all have a secondary level or adult education certifications. Our academic background is from B.A. or Master Degree.

It didn't matter what level of teaching I received, I was always ready. It was challenging teaching a slow student. Some didn't like to study. They came in with a really bad attitude; however, after an hour of teaching them, they changed. They were even willing to participate in a conversation.

At beginning of a new lesson, I introduced the swim or sink method of learning. They were impressed. The following hour they were ready with no negative attitude. I used to start the morning with a famous quotation or idiom. They actually learned those crazy idioms.

Sometimes, I even took a chance of talking about Ebonics. They wanted more......

As every English teacher knows, Ebonics are not taught in the classroom. I taught it because that is the only way students will learn the difference between an idiomatic expression and Ebonics.

Idiomatic expression is mastering the language. Ebonics should be taught to show that it is only street language.

I taught some of my classes through music. A slow student or even an advanced student enjoyed them. Why, because music is the universal language....

After lunch, the students were usually sleepy; therefore, I took them out of the classroom to show them sounds associating them with our environment.

There were many funny and also sad situations in the classroom. I treated each situation with kindness. The students knew that no one was supposed to make fun of the other.

The saddest day for me was retiring from the Language Center. The staff is part of my extended family. The students were my children because I took them with no English what so ever to a fully bilingual individual.

The staff at the Language Center is part of me. I consider them my extended family.

Mr. Eliu Rivera and Myrna Rolon were always there to give me a helping hand when I was going to introduce a new lesson. I learned a lot from them when I went to work there. They had a unique way of teaching. Some students used to tell me that I taught just like Mr. Rivera. Others stated that I even had corny jokes as Ms. Rolon.

Let me also mention Ms. Awilda Quinones, Ms. Nitza Santiago, Mr. Julio Gonzalez, Ms. Gladys Sanchez and Mr. Luis Rivera. They always had kind words for me.

I want to thank my supervisor, Ms. Noris Rodriguez. She was always there when my mom was in the hospital.

When mom died Noris and all the instructors were at my side on that sad day.

My buddies, Iris Quijano and Saul Ortiz went to the cemetery and stayed with me even after my mom was buried.

The military side was also very helpful. They made sure that the warriors treated the instructors with respect.

My thanks to the Puerto Rico National Guard for giving me the opportunity to teach at the Language Center.

Chapter 18

Dolores Rodriguez Quiles
1884-1972

Dolores Rodriguez Quiles was born in 1884 and died in 1972. Who was this lady? Well, she was my great grandmother. She was born in Adjuntas, Puerto Rico. Her father was a Spaniard merchant, Vicente Rodriguez and her mother a high society Spaniard, Lucia Quiles.

Let me take you back in time so that you may get an idea how two young Spaniard met in Puerto Rico and started a family…….

Spanish immigration to Puerto Rico began in 1493 and it continued until 1898. Puerto Rico at that time was a colony of Spain.

On September 25, 1493, Christopher Columbus set sail on his second voyage with 17 ships and 1,200–1,500 men from Cádiz, Spain.

On November 19, 1493 he landed on the island, naming it San Juan Bautista in honor of Saint John the Baptist.

The first Spanish settlement, Caparra, was founded on 8 August 1508 by Juan Ponce de León, born in Valladolid, Spain, a lieutenant under Columbus, who later became the first governor of Puerto Rico.

The following year the settlement was abandoned in favor of a nearby island on the coast, named Puerto Rico, Rich Port, which had a suitable harbor.

In 1511, a second settlement, San German, was established in the southwestern part of the island.

During the 1520s the island took the name of Puerto Rico while the port became San Juan.

The Spanish heritage in Puerto Rico is profound today in its customs and many traditions, language, and in the old and new architectural designs.

The European heritage of Puerto Ricans comes primarily from one source: Spaniards including, Canarians, Asturians, Catalans, Galicians, Castilians, Andalusians, and Basques.

From the beginning of the conquest of Puerto Rico, Castilians ruled over the religious Roman Catholicism and political life. Some came to the island for just a few years and then returned to Spain, however, many stayed.

Among Puerto Rico's founding families were the Castilian Ponce de León family. Their home was built in 1521 by Ponce de Leon but he died in the same year, leaving "La Casa Blanca", or "The White House", to his young son Luis Ponce de León. The original structure didn't last long; two years after its construction a hurricane destroyed it and it was rebuilt by Ponce de León's son-in-law Juan García Troche.

The descendants of Ponce de León's family lived in La Casa Blanca for more than 250 years when in 1779 the Spanish Army took control of it. Finally, the American military moved into La Casa Blanca in 1898.

The southern city of Ponce is named after Juan Ponce de León y Loayza, the great-grandson of the island's first governor.

Immigration to the island caused the population to grow rapidly during the 19th century.

In 1800, the population was 155,426 and ended the century with almost 1,000,000 inhabitants (953,243), multiplying the population by about six times.

The major motivation for the massive European immigration during the 1800s was the Spanish Crown's proclamation of the Royal Decree of Graces of 1815, Real Cédula de Gracias, which led to the arrival of primarily Catholic immigrants from some seventy-four countries.

Puerto Rico, during the 19th century, was very well known to every European country. Among them were hundreds of Corsican, French, Irish, German, Scottish, Italian, Lebanese, Maltese, Dutch, and English and Portuguese families moving to the island.

Some countries were represented by only a few immigrants, i.e., fifty-one Chinese immigrants during this century. The country that still sent the most people was Spain.

From the start of colonization, other groups from Andalusia, Catalonia, Asturias, Galicia, and Majorca had also immigrated, although the Canarian people formed the basis.

Guess what? Once the 19th century came, things changed drastically. According to Puerto Rican authors such as Estela Cifre de Loubriel, who did extensive research on immigration patterns to the island, during the 19th century the greatest number of Spaniards that came to the island with large families were Catalans and Mallorcans.

It is important to know about immigration during that time so that you can visualized what was going in the island during the 18th and 19th.

My great grandparents as many Spaniard, met during family reunions. Since both great grandparents came from a well to do family, it was easy to meet in special events of high society of that era.

My great great-grandfather, Vicente Rodriguez, was 17 yrs. old when he met my great great-grandmother Lucia Quiles. Lucia was also 17 yrs. old.

Both families were very happy when the two love birds announced that they wanted to get married. They knew from the beginning that Vicente and Lucia was a blessed couple.

In June 1883, Vicente and Lucia got married in the Guadalupe Catholic Cathedral of Ponce.

Vicente and Lucia were very happy in Adjuntas, Puerto Rico. They received a piece of land full of crops and a huge house with house keepers. All came from both the Rodriquez and Quiles families. In Ponce; they received stores and a couple of clients from Spain.

After a couple of days after their honeymoon, the newlyweds went to visit their parents......

The families, the Quiles and the Rodriguez, were happy to see the young couple. They wanted to tell them something very important.

The Vicente and Lucia got very anxious. They were surprised to hear that both families wanted to talk to them.

Vicente Rodriguez Sr. told his son that he was returning to Spain. He was going to leave his business in Puerto Rico because in Madrid he had other properties that needed to be taken care.

Lucia's parents had a similar situation. They also had properties in Spain and wanted to go for a visit. They told the newlyweds that they were ready to leave because their son, Vicente Jr. and Lucia, can now run their fortunes in Puerto Rico.....

Vicente and Lucia said their goodbyes to both the Quiles and Rodriguez families. They were very sad because Spain was very far. A trip to Europe took over a month.

During the year that followed, Vicente and Lucia were again blessed. They welcomed their gorgeous child, Dolores Rodriguez Quiles to their loving family.

Dolores upbringing was superb. Since living in Puerto Rico, she acquired a lot of knowledge from the different cultures in the island. Also, she was fascinated because she got the chance of meeting some Tainos Indians.....

Vicente and Lucia decided to relocate to Ponce. It was a great town for merchants. In addition, they kept their coffee and tobacco fields in Adjuntas.

In the town of Ponce, they had their stores and clients. Dolores was doing well in her studies. She had a good head for business.

Dolores was grown up by now. Her parents were now thinking of her future. She had lots of friends both males and females. She told her parents that she wasn't rushing into any marriage at this time.

Vicente and Lucia had other worries. Their parents were in Spain and it wasn't easy keeping in touch with them. Many merchants told them that their parents' business in Europe had double; however, it was getting hard to communicate with Puerto Rico.

Puerto Rico was growing fast not only in their culture, but also it was becoming a mine for commerce.

The politicians were getting scared because at beginning all rules came from Spain. Well to do families knew that they can be elected governors of the island if they wished.

Now....it was getting harder...

Dolores was having fun because her friends were mostly artists, authors, song writers and musicians.

She knew that someday she would get marry, but not now.... Life for her was great....

Dolores parents weren't getting any younger. She was their only offspring. They wanted grandchildren. Both Vicente and Lucia wanted to go to Spain, but they didn't want to leave their daughter.

Dolores told them time after time that she was happy leading the life she was leading. She was aware of her fortune and so were the guys she met. She didn't want to end up supporting any male.

Dolores Rodriguez Quiles, my great grandma, knew Puerto Rico was going through hard times. She kept up with the latest news because her friends told her about the United States and Europe. Things in the island were not the same. Every day something was happening.

The trading with Europe was getting slower. The politicians were facing big threads from the United States.

Finally, it did happen...... the Spanish American War.

During the Spanish-American War, United States forces launch their invasion in Puerto Rico, the 108-mile-long, 40-mile-wide Island that as one of Spain's two principal possessions in the Caribbean was now under fire. With little resistance and only seven deaths, U.S. troops under General Nelson A. Miles were able to secure the island by mid-August.

After the signing of an armistice with Spain, American troops raised the U.S. flag over the island, formalizing U.S. authority over its one million inhabitants.

In December, of the same year, the Treaty of Paris was signed, ending the Spanish-American War and officially approving the cession of Puerto Rico to the United States.

The Spaniard, living in the island, suffered a lot during the war. The well to-do merchants, store owners and high society were getting ready to leave Puerto Rico. The United States informed them that everything they owned will be taken away if they didn't leave.

So....the rich left the island.......

When Dolores' family was ready to relocate to Spain, the hurricane season was about to start.....

On August 8, 1899, Puerto Rico experienced one of the most destructive hurricane in history. It rained for 28 days straight and the winds reached speeds of 100 miles per hour. This was Hurricane San Ciriaco.

The most devastating effect of San Ciriaco was the destruction of the farmlands, especially in the mountains where the coffee plantations were located. San Ciriaco aggravated the social and economic situation of Puerto Rico at the time and had serious repercussions in the years that followed.

The losses of life and property damage were immense. Approximately 3,400 people died in the floods and thousands were left without shelter, food, or work.

Dolores' parents died during the hurricane. They were hit by the heavy storms and their house was washed away.

Nothing happened to Dolores because she was in San Juan visiting some friends....

After Dolores' loss, she had no place to go. The coffee fields and tobacco fields were destroyed....

She tried very hard to locate her grandparents in Spain. They never responded to her many messages. Some merchants told her that it was hard getting information from Spain because the Americans were keeping an eye on them.

Dolores had money in the bank; however, with the change from Spaniard to American money she was left with no money what so ever.

Dolores never gave up. She started going to the seaport trying to get some source of news from Spain.

She didn't succeed… The Americans were all over.…

During those visits to the seaport, that is when she met a young merchant by the name of Amparo Manfredi. This man was very handsome. Dolores hesitated in dating. He kept insisting until she accepted him as her boyfriend.

Dolores was very jealous because Amaparo had a lot of friends. He was only six months in Puerto Rico and the other six at sea. She didn't really know this man. He didn't promise her marriage either. Amparo only told her that he was in love with her.

It was hard to trust someone like him.…

On one of his visit to Puerto Rico in 1904, Dolores told Amparo that she was pregnant. He just looked at her. He stayed long enough to give the baby his name.

Amparo Manfredi Jr. was born on June 10, 1904. He was a very healthy child. Dolores was happy of becoming a mother, but had mixed feeling because Amparo Manfredi Sr. disappeared from her life.….

Once again, Dolores Rodriguez Quiles had to start a new life, and this time with a child.

Slowly DoLores forgot about being Spaniard or anything that had to-do with Spain. She started thinking about her future.

"Bomba y plena" was on her mind…

Dancing was always on her mind even though she was capable of working in any business environment. She wasn't satisfied…

One afternoon, she was looking out her office's window. She saw a couple of wagons. Those wagons had all sorts of signs advertising that they were a traveling theater. They showed up at the port be-

cause many ships stopped in Puerto Rico to leave merchandize from different countries.

Dolores was very curious when she saw the dancers. She thought that it was easier to dance than to sit in an office all day long. She ran down the stairs. Once, outside, she met with the director of the group. She told him that she was a dancer. He greeted her and informed that audition was going to be held in the afternoon.

As she was getting ready to dance, Jose Mercusi was also getting ready to perform.

Jose was the lead dancer of the traveling theater. This theater was made up of dancers and actors from Spain and some locals.

Spaniard valet dancers joined with the "mestizo" in the island. This was a big turn out because when Spaniard and the mestizo worked together the music, songs, dancers and rhythm changed for the best. This is where the Caribbean tone came about.

Dancing was a complete turnaround and I am proud to say that my great-grandmother, Dolores Rodriguez Quiles, was part of that change.

Traditional, folk and popular music did change when the Spaniard mixed with the African.

Some facts about the early music in Puerto Rico:

Music culture in Puerto Rico during the 16th, 17th, and 18th centuries is poorly documented. Certainly it included Spanish church music, military band music, and diverse genres of dance music cultivated by the "jíbaros". The "Jibaros" were the peasants of Puerto Rico.

The "jibaros" or peasants never constituted more than 11% of the island's population, however, they contributed some of the island's most dynamic musical features becoming distinct indeed.

In the 19th century, Puerto Rican music begins to emerge into historical daylight, with notated genres like the "danza". The " danza" was recognized better than the folk genres.

At that time, the "jíbaro" music and "bomba y plena" weren't really documented or recognized as music. I guess it was because of its origin.

The "danza" came from the Spaniard and the jibaro music and "bomba y plena" from the mestizo....

The African people of Puerto Rico used drums made of carved hardwood covered with an untreated rawhide on one side, commonly made from goatskin. A popular word derived from creole to design this drum was "shukbwa", which literally means 'trunk of tree'.

In other islands like Guadalupe, this type of hollowed trunk is called "bwa fuyé".

The classical valet dancers' steps also changed with time....

Jíbaro music

"Jibaros" are small farmers of primarily Hispanic descent. They constituted the overwhelming majority of the Puerto Rican population until the mid-twentieth century. They are traditionally recognized as romantic icons of land cultivation, hard work and self-sufficiency, hospitality, and love of song and dance. Their instruments were relatives of the Spanish "vihuela", especially the *"cuatro"* which evolved from four single strings to five pairs. There is also the lesser known "tiple".

A typical jíbaro group nowadays might feature a "cuatro", guitar, and percussion instrument such as the "guiro" scraper and/or bongo.

Lyrics to "jíbaro" music are generally in the "décima" form, consisting of ten octosyllabic lines in the rhyme scheme abba, accddc. "Décima" form derives from 16th-century Spain.

Although it has largely died out in that country except the Canaries, it took root in various places in Latin America especially Cuba and Puerto Rico where it is sung in diverse styles.

A sung "decima" might be pre-composed, derived from a publication by some literati, or ideally, improvised on the spot, especially in the m of a "controversia" in which two singer-poets trade witty insults or argue on some topic. In between the "décimas", lively improvisations can be played on the "cuatro". This music form is also known as "Tipica" as well as "Tropical".

The décimas are sung to stock melodies, with standardized cuatro accompaniment patterns. About twenty such song-types are in common use.

Explanation of the structure of the "decima".

They are grouped into two broad categories, viz., seis e.g., seis fajardeño, seis chorreao and Aguinaldo.

Aguinaldo:

There are different types of aguildando:
The "Aguinaldo Orocoveño" from the Town of Orocovis
The "Aguinaldo Cayeyano" from the town of Cayes
Traditionally, the seis could accompany dancing, but this tradition has largely died out except in tourist shows and festivals.

Let me explain the "Aguinaldo"

The "Aguinaldo" is most characteristically sung during the Christmas season, when groups of revelers "parrandas" go from house to house, singing jíbaro songs and partying.

The "Aguinaldo" texts are generally not about Christmas, and unlike the Anglo-American Christmas carols, they are generally sung by a solo with the other revelers singing chorus.

In general, Christmas season is a time when traditional music, both seis and Aguinaldo, is most likely to be heard.

Fortunately, many groups of Puerto Ricans are dedicated to preserving traditional music by continued practice.

Jíbaro music came to be marketed on commercial recordings in the twentieth century, and singer-poets like Ramito, Flor Morales Ramos, born 1915 and died in 1990.

All these types of music are well documented, however, jíbaros themselves were becoming an endangered species, as agribusiness and urbanization have drastically reduced the numbers of small farmers in the island. Many "jíbaro" songs dealt accordingly with the changes of migration to New York.

"Jíbaro" music has in general declined accordingly, although it retains its place in local culture, especially around Christmas time, and special social gatherings.

There are many cuatro players, some of whom have cultivated exceptional and unique techniques.

Both of my great grandparents were aware of the change in dancing and melodies throughout the whole island..... Music bought them together. They both knew how to compose, sing decimas and how to dance the "the danza"and "bomba y plena"

Years went by and Jose and Dolores were getting older.... They started working elsewhere....

Jose Mercusi was working as a security guard at the "Matilde" sugar cane fields. He worked night shifts and it was impossible to get a good rest. He was always in a bad mood.

Dolores, in the other hand, kept her other ambition alive. She kept working in hospitals nearby. She acquired a lot of knowledge and graduated as a midwife.

Jose had other things in mind.....

One Sunday morning he told Dolores to iron his best clothing. It was a white jacket and white pants. She cleaned and ironed the suit....

You are not going to believe what happened next.

By midafternoon, the rumors around the neighborhood were that Jose was getting married with Lorenza Sabater...

Dolores was very angry because she was really in loved with this man. They had one daughter, Guadalupe, which he never admitted it was his. He never gave her his last name....

By now, Dolores had two children. The oldest child was Amparo Manfredi Jr. and the youngest Guadalupe Rodriguez.

She was taking classes in "Hospital Damas". This hospital was founded in 1863 as "Santo Asilo de Damas" by Sister Francisca Paz Cabrera. It was attended to by the group known as "Siervas de Maria", Servants of Mary, since 1891.

The hospital was located in downtown Ponce, but on 6 May 1973 it moved to its current location at a new 10-story tower on the north side of the Ponce By-Pass.

The original location of Damas, as the current hospital is commonly called, is now home to Parque Urbano Dora Colón Clavell.

Dolores was always eager to learn more. She was learning from the best nurses in the hospital. She also got involved in delivering babies. That is how she began to study for her licenses as a "partera"

Dolores Rodriguez Quiles graduated as a midwife, "partera". She assisted nurses and doctors in the hospital in order to be certified.

Dolores Rodriguez Quiles never met Mr. Right....

Her last sole mate was Chito Lugo. They had two children Ramon Lugo and Constancia. Guess what? He didn't give Costancia Rodriguez his last name....

Today, after we all watched her blow out the ridiculous number of candles on her 90th birthday cake, my great grandmother looked up at all of us. She was happy to see her children, grandchildren, great grandchildren, and extended family and said, "Look what I started this lovely family. I am so proud to be a part of your lives."

She started telling us her stories.....

Mamá Dolores told us how she did her dancing and singing at "Juan Francisco Sabater Night Club". She worked there only on weekends, because she was taking care of the sick during the week.

Sometimes I say that she was born before her time. Mamá Dolores had the skills of becoming a great physician. She also used to assists the doctor that came to the community once a month.

While waiting for the doctor one afternoon, she decided to write on her journal which was required by law during that time.

On one particular day, she was writing a cure for stomach ulcers. She wrote down how "yerva mora", a plant grown all over Puerto Rico, may cure any stomach virus.

There was a man that was complaining for over a week about the pain. She told him to make tea out of the green plant and add some honey. When the doctor came to visit him, the pain was gone. The doctor informed him to go to the hospital for some analyzes. He did and was diagnosed free of stomach virus or ulcer.

Mamá Dolores was an angel. She didn't charge anyone for her services. She just wished them well. There are so many stories about this wonderful lady.

Mamá Dolores saw Puerto Rico during the Spaniard era and during the invasion of the Americans....

She saw many changes in this beautiful island...

During the first three decades of its rule, the U.S. government made efforts to Americanize its new possession, including granting full U.S. citizenship to Puerto Ricans in 1917 and considering a measure that would make English the island's official language.

Also, during the 1930s, a nationalist movement led by the Popular Democratic Party won wide support across the island, and further U.S. assimilation was successfully opposed.

Beginning in 1948, Puerto Ricans could elect their own governor, and in 1952 the U.S. Congress approved a new Puerto Rican constitution that made the island an autonomous U.S. commonwealth, with its citizens retaining American citizenship.

The constitution was formally adopted by Puerto Rico on July 25, 1952, the 54th anniversary of the U.S. invasion.

The movements for Puerto Rican statehood, along with lesser movements for Puerto Rican independence, have won supporters on the island. However, the popular referendums in 1967 and 1993 demonstrated that the majority of Puerto Ricans still supported their special status as a U.S. commonwealth.

Mamá Dolores used to tell me how different it was during the Spaniard Ruling in this island. She also told me about our ancestors. It was so sad listening to her. Tears were rolling down her cheeks as she told me how she had it all and lost it because of the changed in government…

I never understood her sadness until now My dear "Mamá Dolores" my dear great grandmother, I will never forget you………

Chapter 19

Memories of my grandpa
will last a lifetime

JULIO PAGAN TORRES
10/10/1902-10/10/1964

I wish you were here, but sad to say that you are gone. I still think of your jokes, laughter and your adorable smile. I can remember when you and I used to ride for miles.

When I was six, you would drive me to school.

I thought to myself, "Gosh, riding with "Abuelo", isn't this cool?"

Sometimes we would stop at the candy store where I would get my "piloncitos", but I always wanted you, Papá Julio, to drive a little more so that my friends would see you in your Army uniform…

Papá Julio, I am now grown up and I wish you could see how smart and bright I became.

You lit up my world and put a lot of love in my heart. You helped me with my studies. I still feel you and I know that we aren't very far apart. I know that you are my guardian angel that watches over me.

After all, there is no one else in the world I would rather it be…

I still miss you and wish you were here.

I only have to think of you and shed a big tear.

God had to take you home so you wouldn't suffer any more… You were very sick…

Now you are in heaven and we can't sit on the porch and chat.

I remember all the Army stories and more…

You still live in my heart…

Someday we shall meet again…

Chapter 20

Guadalupe Rodriguez De Pagan
February 12, 1909 -May 13, 1997

"My Abuelita"
Dedicated to my dear grandmother
Guadalupe

If "abuelita" had a meaning
I'll tell you what it would be
If you were close to yours
As mine was close to me

"Abuelitas" are always there
To help you dry your tears
To pamper and spoil you
And conquer all your fears

Even when you did wrong
And all the wrong you'll do
An "abuelita" will always be there
And unconditionally will always love you

My "abuelita" inspired me
To follow my every dream
She would tell me that I wasn't alone

Because we were a team

"Abuelitas" are always busy
And their hearts are very tame
They would tell everyone about you
Everyone would know your name…

"Abuelitas" will keep everything
From when you're young till now
And when you dance or act on stage,
For her you'll take a bow

Without "abuelitas" we would be lost
And our tears would not be dry
We won't be encouraged
To spread our wings and fly

To my "abuelita" I want to say Thank You
You will always be in my heart

MAMA LUPE

What a delight it would be, a heaven with windows…
And guess what? If God granted me a view,
Of all the beauty it beholds, I would only look for you.
I would listen to your laughter that was always
Music to me,
Your beautiful long hair and big brown eyes
is what I would wish most to see.

If I could only SEE you one more time
The smile that warmed my heart,
I would treasure that moment as long as I live and we
must never depart. Here on earth, I look for you
I pray to God for signs,
Every day that passes by, you're still with me in my mind.
I know you're happy in heaven; you've earned
your mansion indeed,

I imagine your kitchen table and you waiting there for me.
I love you and I miss you more than words can say...
What I wouldn't give just to talk to you today.
I hope that you can hear me and listen to my thoughts...
Wherever this life takes me you know
I haven't forgotten you.
Remember, that once upon a time I was
blessed and loved by you, it's true,
Mamá Lupe, if heaven had at least a window
I would only look for you

Chapter 21

The Process of Life

DIGNA MORALES FIGUEROA
AUGUST 25, 1930- DECEMBER 16, 2013

In the following, I will explain;
"What's the process of life?"
Poems dedicated to my dear mother--- Digna Morales Figueroa and to those dealing with aging sickness…

The Process of Life

Lots of people don't want to face the fact that they are getting older. Getting old is just a process and should be appreciated.

Every year we celebrate birthdays. A birthday is the process of aging. So many waste or damage this process by not taking care of their health. When you are eating and exercising properly, you are taking care of the process of life.

Aging is a natural process of life. It begins the moment we are born. Strangely enough, most of us live under the illusion that we and our loved ones will never become old.

When old age arrives, we are often unprepared. The natural order becomes reversed. The young help to care for the old. Those who need to be taken care of for the first time have a hard time accepting that they need help. This condition is a product of our culture that does everything it can to conceal the loss of youth.

Confronting this reality is the beginning of a healthy relationship to life, aging and death.

Dementia

Mother dear, you were dealing with Dementia
You were trapped inside prison walls
That used to be your mind.....
The woman you used to be,
Has long been left behind....

My mother's story

The quiet after the storm: It's raining in Ponce and it's quiet now. The water trickles down the spout and drops are still splattering from the eves. It's soothing. I slept well, better than any night during the last past weeks. A warm glow, an inner peace fills me. I'm content and very happy. I have decided to move with my parents......

By January 2011, I have already settled in my parents' house. My mother was quite happy with my decision.

I had a strange effect of knowing that my mom had Alzheimer. I didn't fully understood what the doctor was telling me, but after the first shock of the news there was a moment of sadness and fear. Then I felt a sudden wave of peace and serenity when I started getting a lot of information about the sickness.

Dealing with this disease alone wasn't easy. My dad is also very sick with diabetes, heart problems, arthritis and many other medical issues that come with age. He was there in the same household, but wasn't much help. I have siblings that I believe didn't care.

Many times, I called my sister and she didn't say anything about coming to Puerto Rico to give me a hand. I had a full time job and it wasn't easy reporting to work with a smile I was an instructor at the National Guard and I always did my job and reported on time.

There were many times that I came home from work and found my dad on the floor. My mom was crying because she didn't know what was going on. They were all day without eating even though I have left lunch in the fridge.

After that incident, I decided to retire from the job I really enjoyed doing. It was a sad decision, but my parents always were first on my list.

The early signs that something was wrong with my mother were subtle.

"She was getting angry a lot. She would go to her neighbor's house without telling me." She also got lost walking down familiar streets.

Her first thoughts after being diagnosed were to just sit and do nothing. "Lying there like vegetables", but the darkness didn't last.

"You can either just roll over or let it come or begin living your life because I am not dead," she told me in the living room.

My whole life changed after I moved with my parents. I made sure I was at her side when she went to see her doctor. He would give me a list of specialists.

They were all very helpful. We became a team. Her primary doctor was the best. He told me one day that if other care takers followed orders from their physician, their love ones will be in better conditions.

Ironically, there are advantages to Alzheimer's. My mother became more focused on what was important to her. She stayed in contact with everybody she loved.

At first, she was afraid of what her friends might say. I was always there with a little humor, and they responded with their continued support.

She still had many ups and downs, which she didn't admit. This disease never stopped me from taking mom shopping or dancing.

In fact, in her good days, she was making plans on coming holidays or events. I gave a monthly journal to her doctor, Dr. Ervin Pacheco Segarra. He was happy with some of the progress she making.

Unfortunately, I want to point out, the incidence of Alzheimer's increases with age. About half the people that reach 80 can expect to get it. Statistics from the Alzheimer's Association confirm this fact.

"This catastrophe could be averted – with more research....There's an answer out there."

For now, I emphasize the value of early diagnosis. It makes all the difference to be prepared and plan the rest of anyone's life.

Knowing what she was up against, I had the time to prepare; mentally, physically, emotionally and spiritually, for what was going to happen.

As soon as she started her medication, the anger stopped. As for brain function, relative to the world, she was still in the normal range, because I started monitoring her behavior.

Mom exercised her mind by playing dominos with my dad and me.

She exercised her body by doing zumba.

My mother, the mother of three, a grandma of four and great-grandmother, still did her chores. She didn't get lost anymore.

She would tell me, "It's strange, but being diagnosed with Alzheimer's has made a profound difference in me for the better!

She would question me "I'm going to die? And then gave me an answer. So what!" I am ready......

She confided, "When I was younger, I was always waiting for or reaching for different goals in life, instead of living in the moment".

She used to tell me that I was the reason for her being alive. I kept her on her toes. There was never a dull moment...

My dear mother died on December 16, 2013 at the age of 83. I miss mom and sometimes I feel as if she is still with me. I smile and keep on doing my daily routine......

I am presently retired and enjoying life. My dad still lives with me. All his ailments are controlled. We go for walks and I keep him eating healthy. At 87, my dad looks great!

Poems to my dear mother
LA DESPEDIDA DE MI QUERIDA MADRE DIGNA MORALES FIGUEROA

25 de agosto del 1930-16 de diciembre del 2013

El alba llegó cuando estaba a tu lado...
Aunque estaba preparada,..... fue fuerte
comprender que tu mi madre querida
Tu espíritu, el soplo, tu alma,
Habían volado alto esa tarde
Del 16 de diciembre 2013 te quedaste para siempre dormida.
Siempre estuve a tu lado...
Yo en tu alcoba con mi padre.
Como siempre solitos contigo.
Tú quieta, inerte, para siempre dormida.
Cerrando tu boquita, acariciando tus manitas,
Mi padre y yo te abrazamos para cubrirte toda.
El llanto, la tristeza larga, el hueco y el vacío,

El dolor que se apodera de tu cuerpo y mente,
Nublando los pensamientos para convertirte
En un ser frustrado e impotente.
La noche nunca se acababa
Escondida detrás de la luna gimiendo

Los días que siguieron fueron todas pesadillas,
Mi llanto se hizo lluvia torrencial,
Mi voz alaridos de espanto,

Sonido de quebranto,
Mi pluma callada,
Y todos los te quiero que muchas veces te dije
Vinieron como ecos
A resonar constantes en mis oídos.
Madre te has marchado aun que estaba preparada
No estaba lista para tu partida
Madre te fuiste dejándome desolada,
Como explicarte mis suspiros por ti
Las veces que me llamaste y yo siempre estuve tiempo para escucharte.
Nunca estuve apurada con mis proyectos
Nunca estuve ocupada con mi trabajo
Tú siempre fuiste primero...
Esa noche del cielo bajo de una nube blanca
De algodón y caramelo,
Un ángel bello vestido de mujer.
Vino a secar mis mejillas de las lágrimas,

Que por ti lloraba madre querida.
Y un desesperante cosquilleo en mi cuerpo
Hizo el recorrido sutil de tus dedos amorosos
Tocaste mi rostro, me tomaste las manos,
y tu voz ronca me repetía:
"no tengas nunca miedo, siempre estaré a tu lado".
Tus manos que fueron las primeras manos que me tocaron cuando nací,

Tus manos que siempre me acariciaron con ternura
Que solo tiene una madre,
Tu compasión por mi dolor cada vez que llorando te contaba
Lo duro del camino, y todo lo que tenía que afrontar.

Cuantas veces tus manos cansadas acariciaron con ternura
Mi rostro de niña

Cuantas veces me dijiste "tu puedes"
Tus versos maravillosos como los del mejor poeta
Encontraron refugio en mis letras,
Ahora que habías partido reparaba en tantas cosas
Que no había acaso comprendido o querido ver.
Madre mis noches se han hecho largas y solitarias
Madre no tengo a quien contarle muchas cosas,
Empiezo a caminar a tu cuarto y entonces recuerdo que ya no estas...

Te extraño tanto, tanto... me haces tanta falta
Eres irremplazable.
Y ahora aprenderé a buscarte en los ojos de
mis hermanos, y de tus nietos,

Y podre encontrarte en mis sueños,
Reconocer tu fragancia,
Guárdalo para siempre en el huerto de mi alma.
Y otra vez la niebla de la noche
Cubrirá mis ojos tristes y cansados,
Y al contemplar el cielo
Al temblar mi frágil corazón partido
Te buscare en las nubes blancas.
Y pasaran muchos de años
Muchos de días, miles de noches.
Y te seguiré amando y buscando en los recuerdos,
Pasaran muchas de noches en que dormida
Iremos de compras a las tiendas,
Al cine, y a la playa,
Cantaremos muchas canciones,
Cocinaremos juntas, y discutiremos,
Y haremos todas las cosas que hacen las madres
Con sus hijas.
Y volveremos algún día a estar juntas

Como cuando me cargabas en tu vientre.
Emprenderé cuando el tiempo me llegue
El vuelo que me acerque a tu lado
Estaremos juntas por fin

Madre e hija,
En paz, amor y armonía
Donde habitan nuestros sueños
Y residen nuestros más fervientes anhelos
Hoy descansas plácida al lado de mi abuela Ceferino
Tu madre...Mi hermano Julio y demás familiares,
Ustedes pueden escuchar nuestras voces
Y en la copa de un árbol celestial llevas
Tu piano con negras, blancas y corcheas
Que se funden en nuestras almas,
En la más hermosa melodía angelical.
Un concierto de sonrisas
Contagiando a las aves
Que emigran a donde levita
La inocencia de las mariposas invernales
y la luz brillante
De nuestras amadas luciérnagas.
Junto a muchos niños vestidos de blanco
Bonitos y angelitos celestiales
Danzando y perfumando todo de jazmines,
Lo que sentimos tus tres hijitos por ti madre,
Que es tan cristalino y puro.

Y hoy, 20 de diciembre 2013...en esta tarde triste de despedida,
Te queremos decir madre querida,
Que estamos rotos y desgarrados
Por el dolor de tu partida,
Que nos haces falta,

Que todos juntos te prometemos
Convertirnos en hombre y mujeres. Justos,
En hermanos amorosos y unidos.
Te llevare conmigo el resto de mi vida
Y sé que en la puerta del cielo
nos estaras esperando
Para recibirnos uno a uno, en tus brazos
Para acariciarnos y limpiarnos
Las heridas de los mortales,
Para llegar a tu lado
Y dormir eternamente
Recostada en paz en tu dulce regazo.

Mother

Mother, you were my faithful companion and confidant even in the most difficult times. You dedicated your life to caring and providing for your four children both physically and emotionally.

You always seem to know how to help us to overcome problems and thrive despite them. Your love was irreplaceable, which made losing you to death an incredibly painful experience.

My Dear Mother
DIGNA MORALES FIGUEROA

When I look up towards the sky
I see birds flying
I see a cloud, the moon, possibly the sun
I can describe lots of things...
When I look up towards the sky

I'll tell you what I see
I see my dear mother
And she's talking to me

She tells me she didn't want to leave me
But it was time for her to depart
It was the hardest thing she had to do
And it's breaking her heart

She tells me I mustn't be sad

Because finally she's pain free
She's found her place in heaven
Underneath a blossom tree

She'll always be there to guide me
When I feel I've lost the way
She'll always be there to comfort me
And wipe those tears away

She'll always be there to share my joy
And laugh at the jokes I make
In order to feel her presence

Only a little imagination it'll take

She may be in the form of a butterfly
Or simply a floating feather
Or hovering over like a busy bee
Or simply part of the weather

On December 16, 2013,
You all came here to say your farewell

But for me it wasn't goodbye
If I want to see her, all I have to do
Is look up towards the sky...

THANKING MY DEAR MOTHER

DIGNA MORALES FIGUEROA
August 25, 1930- December 16, 2013
I will think of you when I see a flower,
The ocean waves, the great vast deep,
You're a beautiful, hidden power.
When day is done, it's time to sleep,
Your memory I'll always keep.....
Thank you, dear Mother.
I will think of you when I see the sunrise,
Clouds run by, the breezes blow,
Then as the days end the color dies,
Memories, thoughts, come and flow,

My love for you more deeply grow,
Thank you, dear Mother.

I will think of you when I see a tree,
With seedlings growing at its skirt,
You loved your family; it's plain to see,
Whether well-dressed, or hands in the dirt,
You healed and comforted every hurt.
Thank you, dear Mother.
I will think of you, watching stars at night,
The great expanse filled with space,
You are an angel shining bright,
Your time on earth was such a grace
In my heart you've a special place

Thank you, dear Mother.
I will think of you when I have some pain,
No one makes it better than you,
Yet how many years you bore the strain,
Of heavy burdens and work to do,
Under your wings we quickly grew,
Thank you, dear Mother.
I will think of you as I'm getting old,
My hair turns slowly gray, then white,
Your courage made me strong and bold,
To face my fears, the dread of night,
Your dear and sweet memories bring great delight.
Thank you, dear Mother.

I will think of you when it's
Time to go,
Home to heaven, our true family,
Your gentle influence will always grow,
You left a treasured legacy,
To help us reach our destiny.

Thank you, dear Mother.
I will think of you when I think of Jesus,
What he says, I'll just repeat,
His gratitude will greatly please us.
I hope to hear him, when we meet.
Thank you, dear Mother.

Mother Dear
DIGNA MORALES DE PAGAN

Today is mother's day and you are gone to heaven…..
I remember that day so clearly…
You were quiet as always you gave me no warning…
Just a sweet smile….
You never said "I'm leaving"
You never said goodbye
You were gone before I knew it,
And only God knew why
After you were gone…

A million times I needed you,
A million times I cried

If Love alone could have saved you,
You never would have died….
I know that someday…
We will be together again...
If you were here today,
We would have been getting ready for
Our celebration…
But today, I am all alone…and could only say,
I love you mom, you will never be forgotten

In Life I loved you dearly
In death I love you still
In my heart you hold a very special place…

FELíZ CUMPLEAÑOS MADRE MIA

Dedicado a mi querida Madre en su
Cumpleaños...

DIGNA MORALES FIGUEROA
25 de agosto del 1930 – 16 de diciembre del 2013

Que lejos están aquellos días
En que cantando alegre y
Jugando con mis hermanos...

Tus primeras caricias, madre mía,
Que desde niña, alegre me
Ofreciste nunca me olvidare...
En el cofre de mi corazón guardo
Aquel ramo de besos que me diste.

Extraño esos dulces consejos...
Extraño tus regaños...

Tú eres la encarnación de la belleza,
el perfume de todos los jardines
y la canción de Dios al infinito....

Chapter 22

My Sister

ADELIN MILAGROS PAGAN MORALES

My dear sister Adelin which I love with all my heart. What can I say about her? Well, like any normal family, we grew up surrounded by lovable parents. My sister is younger than me. We shared everything.

As we got older, we got even closer. We used to talk about boys and friends in general. When it came time to choose a high school, my sister went to the school I went, Prospect Heights H.S.

I used to give her a lot of advices and she did listen. She was a sweet and gentle child. I was the opposite. I guess I was the mother hen to all my siblings.

I recalled one time when a girl came to our block in Brooklyn. She was calling my sister. My parents weren't home. Adelin went downstairs and this girl way older than us wanted to fight. I ran so fast from our apartment to meet this girl.

This young lady came claiming that Adelin was going out with her cousin's boyfriend. I told her to mind her own business. It wasn't my sister fault that the so call boyfriend didn't want her cousin anymore.

Well, guess what? She came forward to hit my sister. That is when I got so angry that I turned into a lunatic on top of that abnormal girl. I warned her not to get close to my sister. She didn't listen.

In the meantime, the other girls around the block came forward. I told them that I can take care of the situation, but to stand by just in case I needed help.

Adelin just stood there crying. I took a stick and was hitting both girls. The two girls couldn't fight back. I beat them badly. They were on the ground for a while. I stopped fighting and they girls ran without a word.

When the fight was over, we went to the corner store for some ice-cream. The owner gave us free milkshakes because he knew those girls were trouble. The whole block congratulated me and the two losers went to Bonds Street with their cloth ripped and messed up hair......

There were a lot of situations where I had to help my sister. I was always there..... Things were no different as adults....

In the following you will see how close we are that is scary.....

I used to think that my sister was part of a Central plan made by God....

It is easy to say that a person has a serious advantage in life if they come from a loving and supportive family. Many people still succeed even though they come from less-than-ideal family situations. By having our basic needs and knowing that our parents loved us, it made it better to cope with all the challenges of day-to-day living. It was much easier to face any obstacle as we grew older.

My sister and I were always coming up with different ideas to help around the house. My mom didn't know how to handle simple every day problem. She used to tell us to wait for our father to come home. We got tired of that answer; therefore, we made our own decisions without telling her.

This was no coincidence. I truly believe that God organized us into families so that we can grow up in happiness and safety. Sometimes I think that we learned to love each other selflessly. It was the key to true joy.

Our neighbors were not surprised that we have graduated from high school with honors and went on to college. My sister, brothers and

I had a dream. That dream came true. It was to finish our education and be ready for the future.

Our family always came first. Perhaps we were one of the lucky ones who were raised in a happy and secure household with two loving parents. Likely, as adults, we wanted the same happy environment for our family. Now a day, living peacefully in a family isn't easy. For us, family values were number One. Those values taught by our parents strengthen our family.

Many people who have lived through disasters never say, "All I could think about during the earthquake was my bank account." They always say, "All I could think about was family." It shouldn't require a disaster for us to know that this is the truth.

When we were growing up, we made a pledge. I reminded my siblings that we were a team. No one would even dare to bother us because we were there for each other.

We made believe that were actors in some sort of a play. I told them to think of the parts we had or will play, in our family role. We looked at all the responsibilities that went along with each one of us. We all put a lot of efforts in put into strengthening our family.

I am saying this because we moved to New York and my parents weren't really ready to raise us there. Things were very complicated in the new environment. In Puerto Rico, my parents had it all.

We were always helping our parents by keeping a peaceful home. We never complain about anything. My sister and two brothers helped me by putting each other's needs first. We never bother to ask for new cloths or toys. All four us learned how to recycle at a very young age. We never got discouraged.

No matter how hard things were we tried to keep our home almost perfect.

I remember one Christmas day that we told our parents that we were happy by just getting hats and gloves as gifts. I promised my sister and brothers that I would save every penny to buy what we really wanted without letting our parents know.

Guess what? We did fine. Since we were so good in school, we all put together a business. I told Papa John that we needed a typewriter to do our school work. I started typing term papers.

My brother Papo did the covers. Julio did some writing and my sister put all the papers together. We made a couple of dollars weekly. We had so much money that we bought leather coats and nice outfits. Sometimes Papa John would borrow from us. He had to payback with interest of course.

As we got older, the boys drifted apart, but my sister and I remained close....

When I got married, Adelin was the one that gave me the money needed for the reception. We both paid for the whole event. We even bought my mother's her dress, shoes and accessories. We paid for the rental of my father's tux.

A couple of years later, Adelin was getting marry. Once again we both paid for everything. We never bother our parents with our problems of monetary expenses. My dad just paid the necessary bills for the house. If my mom needed anything, my sister and I were there to buy it. My mother never asked for much. We spoiled her all the time. My father was happy because he didn't spend anything on my mother.

Even after we got married we took care of our parents. They moved to Puerto Rico and we mailed them packages and money.....

Chapter 23

My Nephews

A person can learn a lot from books, but many things can only be learned the hard way. What do I mean by this? Well, one can learn by living, suffering or even enjoying life. I am sitting here thinking about my family. There were many lessons learned. We were so close and we always took care of each other.

One evening, at approximately, 7 p.m., I was in my room in Ponce. The weather was pleasant; however, it was too quiet. Suddenly, my dogs began to bark. I got worried. I thought that maybe they saw someone trying to break in. If they kept barking, I would have to go downstairs.

I was trying to get up from my bed, but I went down. I thought of the many lessons I've learned in life would end up at the bottom of rubbish or something. I only could tell you that everything in the room started shaking. I couldn't move at all.

A heavy-duty magnetic field was pulling me toward the ground. This weird sensation lasted a couple of minutes. I thought that it was the end of the world. I turned the T.V. on and to my surprise there was a news flash of an earthquake that just hit Puerto Rico. I went to check on my dogs and they were still shivering. They came into the house and I calmed them down. I let them stay on the sofa until morning. I then decided to write what had happened so that my nephews could read it after I am gone. I hope they'll find it useful.

I'm writing this today, April 24, 2016, so that you, Ray and Rebustino, can get an idea that life is too short to waste. There are many reasons why I started writing about the earth shocking event. I feared the earthquake might really destroy me.

All the lessons I've learned in life would have disappeared with me. By writing this, I hope to pass on the few of my memories to you and the rest of my family.

The most important message that I want to bring across is that the vast majority of things you worry about will not bother you the next day. A year later you will not even be able to remember them if you try.

As you got older, you did not worry about what grades you got in high school or college. You are not even worrying about the games you lost when you were in the little leagues.

You won't worry about what other people think about you. Most of the things you worry about now will never happen. Life will still go on no matter what. Please learn to enjoy every day, and try to enjoy it as if it is your last. It has taken me a long time to understand this, and I wish I had understood it sooner.

Happiness is not a destination but a journey. You will never be smart enough, or rich enough. Whatever it is you want, there is always something better.

Enjoy the journey of learning, working, and living. If you enjoy the journey, you'll probably achieve a lot more than if you focused on goals.

If you do decide you want to be "successful", I can give you the formula for success. There are only three things you need to do:

First, decide exactly what it is you want.

Second, determine the price you will have to pay.

Third, and this is the hardest and most important part, pay the price.

Material things don't make you happy, but memories will always stay with you. Whatever it is that you buy, you will soon get used to it. It will make you happy for a short while, but it will not make you happy forever.

I can't even remember most of the toys I've had in my life, but I still think of my times with your mother, my brothers, and your grandparents. Life then was full of happiness. I remember walking with your mother to school and how happy we were. I also remember hugging your grandma when I came home from school. Those memories will never go away.

Your family is the most important thing you have in life. Friends, boyfriends, girlfriends, and co-workers come and go, but the only thing that you can always count on is your family.

If you find a friend who is always there for you, you're extremely lucky. They exist, but they're very rare.

Rebustino, one day, you will have your own family. Ray, you have yours. You guys must love them and look after them. You will understand in the future that just as your grandmother and father died, your mother will die as well. Strive to be good sons.

Don't be surprise if one day, you will be like your parents. Your parents were not perfect, and you will not be either, but you can be loving and good.

Never stop learning, and always be ready to teach yourself things you don't know. The only things you will remember are things you care about. No one can teach you everything you need to know. You will also forget most of what you study, and that is fine.

Remember to always stay curious, and you'll be surprised how much you can learn. Let me tell you something that when people speak of intelligence, what they generally mean is curiosity. All great discoveries start with a question. Children are born curious, and school can beat it out of you. Never stop asking questions.

Ray and Rebustino, you're never too old to learn. I want you two to promise me that you are never going to live someone else's life. Find your gifts and the things that give you pleasure, develop those gifts, and pursue them.

Do what makes you happy and be great at it. You have skills and gifts that no one will ever have or see again.

I think that's very important when you learn how to cope in life. Once you learn how, you'll want to change it and make it better.

It is up to you do decide whether you will be strong or not. Many people suffer great tragedies and live full and happy lives. Remember the people you love.

Accept those terrible things that may happen. Try to live as if each day is your last with those you love. There is nothing else you can do.

At this time, I want to thank you both for letting me be part of your lives. You both gave me a chance to be not only your aunt, but also your second mother. Sometimes I laugh at the things we did together. I always looked forward to each of your birthdays, little leagues games, school plays, graduations and much more.

I remember very clearly those summer days in Massapequa. We used to be at the pool very early. You guys were taking swimming lessons. I was very impressed when within days you both learned how to swim.

I was always present at every birthday party. Your mother and I would pick up a theme to decorate the basement or park. As always, I was the clown. I believe I had more fun than the kids....

There were other funny occasions that I remember clearly. Rebustino and I went to see lots of movies. After each show, we would go to a restaurant. Rebustino was a perfect gentleman. While eating, we would chat about the movie. We went to see the Titanic, The Mask, and The Flintstone just to name a few. I really enjoyed every moment spent with you two.

Sometimes your parents would go out and I stayed babysitting. We played with your Nintendo, electronic bowling machine and even yatzee.

I hope you still remember those happy times, because I will never forget them....

Chapter 24

My brothers: Juan José Pagán Morales
Julio Manuel Pagán Morales

On one cloudy humid summer afternoon, in Brooklyn, we were walking toward the park. One could feel the hot air. It was as if the air was carrying some dusty smell as a result of the earlier rainfall. I do like the raindrops, but not when it was time to go to the park. Sometimes when I was studying, it used to break up my concentration.

When the rain stopped, my sister and I took a chance to walk to the park. We saw my mom peered out of the window. Her attention was drawn to my father's car.

There were people sitting out there and the car was their main sitting bench. She wondered if any of them was responsible for the broken side mirror on the passenger's side. Wild imagination my mother had. She thought and quickly cleared her mind of that. She went back to her house chores.

Before she could go back to her cleaning, something her father used to say came upon her mind. My mother could hear those words as loud as her father had said them. "My children take education serious and secure a bright future." My mom gently shut her eyes and nodded in appreciation of that advice.

My parents were proud of their four children because all of us studied hard and were very good in sports. That is why they let us go to the park to practice volleyball.

My mother promised her father that her children would go to college.... "Papá, I will," she said to herself in a low tone and went back to her cleaning.

Juan and Julio were punished as always......

My brothers, who were younger, had examinations in a month's time. They were not allowed to leave the house.... As each day passed and drew the examination day closer, Juan burned with the enthusiasm to read and excel, while Julio simply whiled away his time.

He was always going out, chatting with friends, engaging in friendships that spared him no time for studies.

My sister and I always did our assignments on time even though we had sport practice. My two brothers always tried to get us in trouble, but they never succeeded.

One day after school, an appealing aroma diffused from the pot of soup our mother had finished making. My brothers didn't want to eat because my mother wasn't that great as a cook.

"Your culinary skills are unquestionable," Julio said to my mother, laughing.

"I have to make sure my family eats well," replied our mother.

"How are you getting on with your studies, Juan?" She asked.

"Well, I am doing my best, which I hope will see me through," was Juan's quick reply. My mom was impressed.

"A good education is quite essential if one desires a sound foundation in life," she said. "You don't know how much I still wish my own parents knew the worth of education and had given me a chance," she further said and looked up. In her eyes was lots of regret. Juan sensed it, and quickly turned to his mother.

My mom always blamed her mother for not finishing school. My grandfather died when mom was four years old. She always told me that her father used to talk to her. I reminded her that he was dead.....

"Everything will be just fine," said Juan. "I will strive to be all you and Papí never had a chance to do," he further spoke to pacify our mother.

Juan saw a smile flash on my mother's face, brightening it. Then it dulled again with a maze of wrinkles so pronounced.

"What is it again "Mamí"?" The disturbed Juan asked.

"I'm just worried that you are a hardworking individual, but Julio, your brother is not." Juan chuckled.

"Don't worry," "Mamí". I will talk to Julio," said Juan, believing he could bring his influence to bear on Julio towards reversing his attitudes to his studies.

Julio tickled with awareness that someone had come into his room, but did not bother to turn around to find out who it was. He was lying down. His books were on a wooden table, begging and yearning to be read, when Juan entered.

The first glance Juan threw fell on Julio, and then on his books – those that he had not touched for a long time had gathered enough dust, and had become full of spider cobweb. It was all an ugly sight to Juan; most especially seeing Julio lie aimless and staring at the walls. He could not help getting worried.

Juan sat beside Julio. "Are you trying to sleep or meditating?" He gently asked. Julio sat up. He starred at Juan as if he was a shrink or a stranger that had come to bother him.

There was something aggressive about Julio's glare on Juan. It nailed him with intense ferocity.

"No I'm not", Julio who was very good at punning, "but why are you so concerned?" He demanded.

"Look, Julio," Juan said, wanting to say all he meant before Julio's interruption.

"You have nothing else to do? And you have come here to look at my face," said Julio. His tone began to rise.

"You must listen to me, Julio."

"What is it, Juan? Say it fast and briefly! I am not in the mood to entertain a speech!"

Juan was determined to bring about a change of attitude in his brother. He allowed a wide smile light up his face before sitting closer to him. Julio appeared to have lost a bit of his earlier aggressiveness.

There was, however, a sneering look on his face that was so determined not to give way for a smile. No matter how hard Juan tried.

"Alright, my tough brother", Juan began, "what is your problem?"

"And you think as my older brother, the solution is with you?"

"You answered my question with a question, Julio. You have said nothing."

"My problem, you want to know?"

"Yes you are my brother and I should be distressed when all is not well with you."

"Thank you so much. Thank you so much for caring. I have no problem."

"You can't say that, Julio. It is clear you are not focused in your studies."

"When did you become my mentor? I can't remember hiring anyone."

"We are not here for jokes, Julio."

"Jokes? Well, Juan, you met me lying down. I was thinking about life."

Juan immediately realized when Julio made it easier for him to express the real contents on his mind. He wasted no time at all in demanding why Julio never took his studies serious, in a slow soothing tone that carried all the love and concern for his dear brother.

"And yet you made us believe you want to be a doctor," said Juan. "Please don't come to believe anything good can be achieved without hard work."

Juan offered to help Julio out of his predicament, but he was in no mood to further listen to him. There was a sneering look on Julio's face that fully portrayed his resentment.

"Are you through?" He asked, holding back his simmering anger. Juan uttered not a word, but looked on.

"Leave me alone," Julio added in a harsh tone of voice. He gave Juan no other chance. All his proposals were yelled down.

Though that was a big shock for Juan, he shrugged his shoulders and left, fully filled with the feeling that he had done his best and what he ought to do. Not even their mother was impressed with Julio's behavior. Not even words of advice showered on Julio by invited elders could change him.

To worsen matters, a relationship ignited between Julio and José. José was a boy whose questionable behavior was being frowned at by every right-thinking person in our building.

His romance with the streets were a known fact. Rumors did the rounds; Julio was warned to stay off that friendship, but again it was synonymous to pouring water into a basket.

My mother cried often, and Juan always consoled her, by telling her to believe all would be well at the end.

The examination day eventually came. Juan received it with a lot of confidence. His hopes were high. It was clear to him as crystal that he was quite prepared. He however, made requests to his inspire-rational creator for further assistance. Julio on his part was never really understood.

Expectations were really common. He kept everyone wondering why he even bordered to sit for the examination.

A lot of caring people anticipated a surprise. Many erroneously believed that he could do it. Some believed he secretly prepared for the exam. A lot of hands were kept crossed.

Not even Felix, Julio's friend, could convince him to prepare adequately for the test. Julio paid Felix a visit one evening. Then, only one hundred and forty four hours separated him from taking the examination.

"I don't have any peace of mind in that house," Julio complained to Felix during one of their several discussions. "Every now and then, it is study or you don't study seriously or well enough. Felix wished he were in Julio's shoes.

"What your mother and brother are saying is not bad at all," he remarked to Julio's disappointment. Julio had thought Felix would support him.

"It is in your best interest and they obviously want the best for you," Felix further said.

"And what is that supposed to mean?" Julio thundered.

"I will always tell you the truth as a friend," said Felix.

"Meaning what? I will go to park and make out something." Julio shouted again.

"How I wish I have such a backing now at your disposal," Felix said to Julio.

At the end of their discussion, Julio's friendship with Felix hit the rocks.

"Listen Felix, I thought you were a friend. Now I know better," were Julio's harsh words before he stormed out.

It took a couple of months for the examination results to be released. Many like Juan were successful. He was accepted at Art and Design in New York. It was a dream come true for Juan, who for a long time had dreamt of studying there. A school he had not been to, but was full of mental pictures out of what he had heard about it.

-

The hustle and bustle of the city: its high-rise buildings in Manhattan were waiting for Juan. There was hunger in Juan to see the school and new friends.

"At last!" screamed Juan, who jumped into the air severally in celebration. "Papí said it. So did Mamí that hard work pays. Art and Design, here I come!"

Julio had nothing to show. His careless attitude to his studies guaranteed that he came off with the worst result of the examination. That laid to rest all speculations that he could spring a surprise.

It was when the big and demeaning examination failure became Julio's goal on going to Brooklyn Tech more seriously. He was ashamed of his performance, and surprisingly sad. Now, it was too late to cry. Confusion set in, got bigger. If only he could turn back the hands of time.

Even the wind carried Juan's outstanding performance. His mother was thrilled, though her joy was with pains of sadness as a result of Julio's score.

Juan rolled from one end of his bed to the other, in excitement every night. Julio stayed awake most nights. He whispered out of untold frustrations, stared hard also at the walls in his room. There were enough dried tear marks that had already defined his handsome face.

"If only I had realized my acts were misleading," he uttered in an almost lifeless tone of regret.

Juan counted the days and prepared for his first day in school. His excitement became bigger, fourteen days to the day of the new semester. He chose to represent the remaining days with short straight lines on sand. A line he cleaned off as each day aged and was gone. Twice he stayed out late into the night, watching the moon, imagining himself as a qualified artist.

Meanwhile, Julio was deep down in sorrow......

The day for Juan's big day came at last. There was slight breeze on that autumn morning, which resulted not in rainfall. The sun had risen to warm up the remarkable day by the time Juan was ready to leave.

He didn't sleep much the previous night. He was full of excitement. That same night, Julio cried all through. He would have cried a river if it were possible. His self-afflicted sorrow occasionally broke into Juan's joy, but there was nothing he could do.

Juan left his home in a happy mood. Even the dogs wagged their tails as he was leaving.

A year has gone by after Juan had started studying at Art and Design. Julio had another chance to take the entrance examination for Brooklyn Tech. He also found himself in the school of his dreams.

But guess what? He had problems. He never spoke to our parents, to me or my sister. Those years further sank him in shame. At a point, he even wished the earth could open up and swallow him.

José paid Julio a visit one sunny and bright afternoon. Julio was downcast when he stepped in.

"Thanks goodness I had a feeling I may not found you home," said José.

"Where would I go?" Julio asked, "As wounded as I am! I love your jacket, José," Julio remarked, as a little smile flickered on his face.

"Thanks," José responded in delight. "I would have been amazed if you did not have at least one compliment for it. It costs a lot to dress up these days."

"You look absolutely great, José," Julio announced, "You amaze me a lot. How do you get to look so elegant with your salary?"

José smiled and sat beside Julio.

"This is going to be an afternoon of a thousand questions. It's simple," said José.

"How? You look expensive. How do you make all the money? You are not telling me something, José."

José grinned. "It's very easy," he quietly said to Julio. "Just as counting 1, 2, 3."

"Now what are you talking about?" Julio who was all lost quickly asked.

"Just with a bit of intelligence, smartness, and good looks, you are there. Your clients will be all over you."

Julio remained puzzled, and completely out of touch with José's points.

"What kind of clients?" He asked timidly, showing his naivety.

"Oh, Julio, don't tell me you don't know what I'm talking about."

"José, I don't, and to be sincere. What is it?"

"Now, let me call a spade a spade. It's all about being a good sales person. Drugs are the name of the game."

"But why?" Julio asked with some disgust, which José noticed.

"I don't blame you," José responded. "You will remain in this building until you get old. You don't have to look this miserable."

"You are wrong, José. I won't remain like this."

"Listen well. You are blessed with great looks and talent. You can get lots of money."

"What about my dignity as a young man?" Julio asked. "Must I throw it to the wind?"

José laughed briefly and got up. He looks at Julio and smile.

"Who talks about that today?" he questioned hard "Dignity my foot. All that matters is to make some money. Money and just money!"

"Anyway? Any way or any how you make it?"

"How you make it is of no consequence, Julio. Be smart. Wake up! You can even buy your own house."

"Really?" Julio screamed out of excitement. "Tell me more," he demanded.

But José told him no more. He just stood there demanding an action with words on Julio's part.

Julio walked with José to the door and told him that he never wanted to see him ever again………

Brooklyn Tech was all Julio had heard all his life. He knew that he was smart enough to make in life. Julio was determined to make his family proud of him.

After being accepted at Brooklyn Tech, Julio was happy once again. He still wanted to make more changes in his life. So, one afternoon right after school, Julio went to enlist in the military. He decided to go in and to everyone's surprise, he took the test and passed. He had to choose which branch in the military he was best qualified.

The recruiter told him that he scored very high. Julio didn't hesitate to go into the Air Force. My father was very happy. Julio had grown up to be a very responsible person.

My mom was crying because she didn't want any of her children in the military. She recalled the many times my dad and grandpa were off to war. He told my parents that the Air Force would help him with his college tuition and future goals.

While in the Air Force, Julio kept studying music and voice training as elective courses. Military was great too. He became a sergeant. He was already there serving his country for years.

After eight years of service, he decided to leave. He took a test for the post office. He was hired immediately He enjoyed that job because he had a chance to study counseling and also in the field of social worker. Life was great at this point for Julio.....

Julio never gave up his dream.... He didn't become a doctor, but he made a lot of people happy with his singing.

I forgot to mention that even though Julio wasn't married, he had a son.

Julio Manuel Pagan Morales
May 22, 1954 - September 19, 1998

Flashbacks of Yester...Years
In memory of my brother Julio M. Pagan
As I look out the window...
On this summer day, my mind wanders
And think of summer passed.
Days when we were young.
It seems like only yesterday...
It makes me sad.

I miss the freedom of our youth.
I miss long walks to Dairy Queen
Down Court Street passed St. Mary's church...
Walking around eating ice cream.
Simple conversation, Laughter
And sharing between brothers and sisters.
We were a team ... Years have changed us

And our lives different directions... They sometimes
Move closer and other times apart…
I never thought that I would miss the times we shared.

Thinking that our lives will always intertwine.

Juan also made his dream come true. He became a Police Officer in the NYC. He also made us proud by becoming a detective. He served twenty years in this second to none organization. He is now retired; however, he is keeping up with his art work.

He is married, has one daughter, and three grandchildren……

Chapter 25

My Mother and her In-laws

When my parents said I do,
they became part of each other family;
Often the transition was hard,
and a lot of hostility.

They often found it hard to be accepted,
The in laws for what they were;
Some were mean and some were nice,
Some were plain bizarre.

For my mother that wasn't the case,
She loved them right from the start;
My grandparents were great,
Full of love with generous hearts…

They always made her truly feel,
That she was indeed their daughter;
Around them she was always safe,
And together they always had fun.

My mom used to say,
That she wouldn't trade them,

For money, silver or gold;
For she was blessed with the best…

My mother died on December 16, 2013. I wasn't a bit surprised when the only family at the funeral was her in laws…..

Kike and his wife Migdalia came to my house the minute they heard about my mom.

Julio Pagan Rodriguez, my uncle, was present at the funeral. He spoke on both the funeral and the cemetery. He told stories about my parents.

I will never forget how my uncles and aunts on my father's side came to give me full support….

My mom and Julio were in school together. They had the same teacher. She told me how he used to bother her and little did they know that they were going to be in-laws.

When we moved to New York, my dad started helping his family. My mom never said anything. She was always willing to help my grandparents and all my uncles and aunts.

Julio moved to New York and lived in our tiny apartment for a couple of months. My dad helped him get a job at Livingston Factory. My mom went around the neighborhood to see if there was an apartment available.

She found one not too far from us. My uncle was happy because he wanted to bring his family to New York.

Years went by and my father and uncle took the test for the transit department in New York. My father and uncle passed the written test. They were sent to take a medical examination. Everything was going well; however, my father gave too much information. He told the examiner that he had an old injuring in one hand. When the examiner saw it, my father was disqualified…..

My uncle Julio Pagan Rodriguez began working for transit in 1969. My father had to keep his old job….

Chapter 26

Vicente Pagan Rodriguez

My dear uncle
9 November 1948 - 27 February 2015

My uncle and I grew up together. We were always playing and getting in trouble.

When we were just on primary grades, I was always defending him, why? Because my uncle was a sweetheart. He never did any harm.

The kids in our class used to bother us because he was dark, and I was light complexion. My response was always the same. I used to reply to those fools that I was born in the daytime and my uncle at night.

The teasing got so bad that I used to fight with a stick or just plain punches. My uncle didn't want to fight.

One day as we were walking down the street of New York City. A white-haired old man begged us for money. My uncle, Vincent, gave him a quarter. Noticing my surprised look and he said:

"That poor unfortunate reminds me of a story which I will tell you, the memory of which continually pursues me.

My uncle and I were always telling stories. We were the story tellers of the class.....

Uncle began his story:

"My family, which came originally from Ponce PR, was not rich. We just managed to make ends meet. My father worked hard, came home late from the National Guard, and earned very little. I had two sisters and seven brothers.

"My mother suffered a good deal from our reduced circumstances. She often had harsh words for my father, indirect and clever reproaches. The poor man then made a gesture which used to distress me. He would pass his open hand over his forehead, as if to wipe away perspiration which did not exist.

He would answer nothing. I felt his helpless suffering. We economized on everything, and never would accept an invitation to dinner, so as not to have to return the courtesy.

All our provisions were bought at bargain sales. My sisters made their own dresses. My brothers shared their clothing, and I had old worn out rags.

The price of food was very high. Meat and fish were only eaten on Sundays. Our meals usually consisted of rice and beans, prepared with every kind of sauce invented by my mother.

She kept telling us that the food was healthy and nutritious, but I should have preferred a change.

"I used to go through terrible scenes on account of lost buttons and torn pants."

"Every Sunday, dressed in our best, we would take our walk along the breakwater. My father, in his Army uniform. He would offer his arm to my mother and they would walk very proud with all nine of us. My sisters, who were always first, would walk ahead of us.

My sisters marched arm in arm. They were of marriageable age and had to be displayed. I walked on the left of my mother and my father on her right.

I remember the arrogant air of my poor parents in those Sunday walks, their stern expression, their stiff walk. They moved slowly, with a serious expression, their body's straight, and their legs stiff, as if something of extreme importance depended upon their appearance.

"Every Sunday, when a ship was returning from unknown and distant countries, my father would always say the same words:

"'What a surprise it would be your grandfather were on that one! Eh?'

"My grandfather, my dad's father, was the only hope of the family, after being its only fear. I had heard about him since childhood, and it seemed to me that I should recognize him immediately, knowing as much about him as I did.

I knew every detail of his life up to the day of his departure for New York, although this period of his life was spoken of only in hushed tones.

"It seems that he had led a bad life, that is to say, he had wasted his money, which action, in a poor family, is one of the greatest crimes. With rich people a man who amuses himself is generally called a sport.

But among needy families, a boy who forces his parents to break into the capital becomes a good- for-nothing rascal. This distinction is just, although the action is the same, for consequences alone determine the seriousness of the act.

Well, Grandpa Juan had visibly reduced the inheritance on which my father had counted on. Then, he moved to New York.

Once there, my grandpa began to sell something or other. Soon he wrote that he was making a little money and that he was going to be able to help my father.

This letter caused a profound excitement in the family. My grandpa, who up to that time, had not been worth anything suddenly became a good man, a kind-hearted fellow, true and honest like the rest of the family.

One captain of a ship told us that grandpa had rented a large shop and was doing well...

Two years later a second letter came, saying: 'My dear Julio, I am writing to tell you not to worry about my health, which is excellent. Business is good. I leave tomorrow for a long trip to South America. I may be away for several years without sending you any news. If I shouldn't write, don't worry.

When my fortune is made, I shall return to Puerto Rico. I hope that it will not be too long and that we will all live happily together . . . .'

This letter became the gospel of the family. It was read all the time. It was shown to the whole town.

For ten years nothing was heard from Grandpa Juan; but as time went on my father's hope grew, and my mother often said:

"'When grandpa gets here, our position will be different. There is one who knew how to get along!"

So, every Sunday, while watching the big ships approaching from the horizon, pouring out a stream of smoke, my father would repeat his eternal question:

"'What a surprise it would be if your grandpa were on that one! Eh?"

"We almost expected to see him waving his handkerchief and crying: "'Hey! Julio!"

"Thousands of schemes had been planned on the strength of this expected return; we were even to buy a little house with my grandpa's money - a little place in the country near Ponce.

In fact, I wouldn't swear that my father had not already begun negotiations.

My eldest sister was then eighteen, the other one sixteen. They were not yet married, and that was a great grief to everyone.

At last a suitor presented himself for the younger one. He was a clerk, not rich, but honorable. I have always been morally certain that grandpa's letter, which was shown to him one evening, had swept away the young man's hesitation and definitely decided to marry my youngest sister.

He was accepted eagerly, and it was decided that after the wedding the whole family should take a trip to New York.

My sister's wedding was very simple. Only immediate family attended the celebration. My father told everyone that once we return from New York, we shall have the biggest wedding celebration ever....

New York is the ideal trip for poor people. It is not far; one crosses a strip of sea in a ship and lands on foreign soil, as this little island is a Common Wealth of the U.S. Thus, as a Puerto Rican, with a ten hours' sail, can observe the neighboring people at home and study their customs.

This trip to New York completely captivated our ideas. It was our sole anticipation and the constant thought of our minds.

At last we left. I see it as plainly as if it had happened yesterday. The boat was getting up steam; my father, puzzled, was supervising the loading of our three pieces of baggage.

My mother, nervous, had taken the arm of my unmarried sister, who looked lost since the marriage of my other sister. She was acting like the last chicken on the farm.

Behind us came the bride and groom, who really wanted to be alone. My older brothers were just playing around. They didn't care what was going on.

The whistle sounded. We got on board, and the vessel, leaving the breakwater, forged ahead through a sea as flat as a marble table. We watched the coast disappear in the distance, happy and proud, like all who do not travel much.

My father was swelling out his chest in the breeze, beneath his sport jacket that was washed that morning. He spread around him that odor of detergent which always made me recognize Sunday.

Unexpectedly, he noticed two elegantly dressed ladies to whom two gentlemen were offering oysters. An old, ragged sailor was opening them with his knife and passing them to the gentlemen, who would then offer them to the ladies.

They ate them in a dainty manner, holding the shell on a fine handkerchief and advancing their mouths a little in order not to spot their dresses. Then they would drink the liquid with a rapid little motion and throw the shell overboard.

My father was probably pleased with this delicate manner of eating oysters on a moving ship. He considered it good form, refined, and, going up to my mother and sisters, he asked:

"'Would you like some oysters?"

My mother hesitated on account of the expense, but my two sisters immediately accepted. My mother said in a provoked manner:

"I am afraid that they will hurt my stomach. Offer the children some, but not too much, it would make them sick." Then, turning toward me, she added:

"'As for Vicente, he doesn't need any. Boys shouldn't be spoiled.'"

I remained next to my mother, finding this discrimination unjust. I watched my father as he arrogantly conducted my two sisters and his son-in-law toward the ragged old sailor.

The two ladies had just left, and my father showed my sisters how to eat them without spilling the liquor. He even tried to give them an example, and seized an oyster. He attempted to imitate the ladies, and immediately spilled all the liquid over his sport jacket. I heard my mother mumble:

"He would do far better to keep quiet."

Abruptly, my father appeared to be worried; he retreated a few steps, stared at his family gathered around the old shell opener, and quickly came toward us. He looked very pale, with a peculiar look. In a low voice he said to my mother:

"'It's extraordinary how that man opening the oysters looks like my father Juan."

"Surprised, my mother asked:

"Who? Your father?"

My father continued:

"Why yes, my father. If I did not know that he was well off in New York, I should think it was him."

Confused, my mother hesitated:

"'You are crazy! As long as you know that it is not him, why do you say such silly things?"

But my father insisted....

"'Go on over and see for yourself Lupe! I would rather have you see with your own eyes."

She got up from her chair and walked to her daughters....

In the meantime, I was also was watching the man. He was old, dirty, wrinkled, and did not lift his eyes from his work.

My mother returned and I noticed that she was trembling. She exclaimed quickly.

"I believe that it is him. Why don't you ask the captain? But be very careful that we don't have this mam on our hands again!"

My father walked away, but I followed him. I became strangely moved.

The captain, a tall, thin man, with blond whiskers, was walking along the bridge with an important air as if he were commanding a presidential ship.

My father addressed him ceremoniously, and questioned him about his profession, adding many compliments.

"'What might be the importance of going to New York? What did it produce? What was the population? The customs? The nature of the trip?" etc., etc.

"You have there an old, the shell opener, who seems quite interesting. Do you know anything about him?"

The captain, whom this conversation began to bore him, answered dryly,

"He is some old Puerto Rican who I found last year in New York. I brought him back home. It seems that he has some relatives in Ponce, but that he doesn't wish to return to them. He claims that he owes them money. His name is Juan, Juan Pagan or Torres or something like that. He told me that he was once rich, but as you can see, that is what's left of him now."

My father turned ashy pale. He became speechless. He was so ashamed of this man. My father's face showed lots of sorrow. After a few minutes he turned to the captain and said:

"'Ah! Ah! Very well, very well. I'm not in the least surprised. Thank you very much, captain."

"He went away, and the amazed sailor watched him disappear. He returned to my mother very upset that she said to him:

"'Sit down; someone will notice that something is wrong.'

"He sat down on a bench and paused:

"'It's him! It's him!'

"Then he asked:

"'What are we going to do?'

"She answered quickly:

"'We must get the children out of the way. Since Vicente knows everything, he can go and get them. We must take good care that our son- in-law. He doesn't have to find out".

"My father looked absolutely confused. He murmured.

"'What a tragedy!'

"Unexpectedly growing furious, my mother exclaimed.

"'I always thought that thief would never do anything, and that he would never drop down on us again! As if one could expect anything from a Pagan!'

"My father passed his hand over his forehead, as he always did when his wife reproached him. She added,

"'Give Vicente some money so that he can pay for the oysters. All that it needed to cap the climax would be to be recognized by that beggar. That would be very pleasant! Let's go to the other end of the boat, and take care that man doesn't come near us!'

"They gave me five dollars and walked away.

"Amazed, my sisters were waiting for our father.

I told them that mama got a sudden attack of sea-sickness. I went to see the shell opener and asked him:

"'How much do we owe you, sir?'

"I wanted to laugh he was my grandpa! He answered.

"'Two dollars and fifty cents.'

"I held out my five dollars and he returned the change. I looked at his hand; it was a poor, wrinkled, sailor's hand, and then I looked at his face, an unhappy old face. I said to myself:

"'That is my grandpa, my dad's father, my grandpa!'

"I gave him a ten-cent tip. He thanked me:

"'God bless you, my young man!'

"He spoke like a poor man receiving a donation. I couldn't help thinking that he must have begged over there! My sisters and brothers looked at me, surprised at my generosity. When I returned the two dollars to my father, my mother asked me in surprise.

"'Was there two dollars and fifty cents worth? That is impossible.'

"I answered in a firm voice...

"'I gave him a tip.'

"My mother started staring at me, she exclaimed:

"'You must be crazy! Giving a tip to that man, to that bum".

"She stopped at a look from my father, who was pointing at his son-in- law. Then everybody was silent.

"Before us, on the distant horizon, a purple shadow gave the impression that something was rising out of the sea. It was New York.

"As we approached the breakwater a violent desire held me once more to see my grandpa Juan, to be near him, to say to him something consoling, something tender.

But as no one was eating any more oysters, he had disappeared, having probably gone below to a dirty room which was the home of the poor old man."

My uncle and I made up so many stories that our English teacher told us that we should write them. It was easy for my uncle and me to be so talented. I believe that we got that from our ancestors....

I miss my uncle a lot.....

As I sit here writing, memories of the many parties and my own prom came to mind. My uncle Vicente took me to my prom and a lot of other parties. Since we were only two months apart, we had the same friends.

Some of our stories were not all made up. The following were real situations that happened to my uncle and me. These are very amusing.

My father and grandfather came from drill one Sunday afternoon. They brought home small parachutes. Vicente called me right away. He kept telling me that one was for me and another one for him....

As we were climbing the balcony, my grandfather ran towards us. He hugged us and didn't get angry. My grandfather was really angry at my dad. He yelled at him because he took those parachutes.

Those small parachutes were used to drop food and supply from the plane to the fields. He reminded my father that all supplies were to be used during drill and not to take anything home....

When my uncle Vicente and I were in grammar school, we were always doing our homework together. It got to a point that we couldn't work alone.

We couldn't keep quiet either. So, the teacher kept us apart. She also called my parents and told them about the situation. I was transferred to another school and he dropped out of school.

He started working in a factory. The pay was very low. I kept telling him that he was too smart to work there.

During the early 70's, my uncle was drafted. He decided to join the Army. Right after basic and advance training, he was sent to Germany.

I forgot to mention that my uncle got his H.S. diploma and used his G.I. bill to further his education. I was so proud of him. Many didn't believe in him. They only said that he was no good, but I knew better.

Let me remind you that when he returned to New York from Germany, he worked in the Police Department. He did an outstanding job there as a Motor Vehicle Operator. He then decided transfer to Transit Department for City of New York.

He was an outstanding soldier and city worker until he was diagnosed with cancer. My uncle never gave up. He went to the best doctors. He was a cancer survivor for almost sixteen years....

R.I.P. my dear uncle. You will never be forgotten.

Chapter 27

Liduvina Perez Echevarria

<u>The emotional impact of a person living with cancer</u>
<u>Liduvina's first reaction…</u>

She told us about her visit to the doctor…
Liduvina began her story like this: "There is a fear that goes through you when you are told you have cancer. It is so hard at the beginning to think about anything but your sickness. It is the first thing you think about every morning.

I want people living with cancer to know it does get better. Talking about it helps you deal with all of the new emotions you are feeling. You have to follow your doctor's orders. Remember, it is normal to get upset."

When Liduvina was told she had cancer, she thought her life was over. This was about ten years ago. She started thinking about her family. The sad part was that she only concentrated on how her family was going to take it. She didn't think twice about taking care of her sick mother.

Once she told me that she was feeling great. Sometimes she missed her appointments just to be with her mom. Her mother died in April 2014.

Liduvina kept talking about her sickness….

The bad thing about cancer is that it affects not only you, but also your family. You may feel scared, uncertain, or angry about the unwanted changes cancer will bring to your life. Sometimes you may feel numb or confused. You may also have trouble listening to, or remembering what people tell you during this time.

This is especially true when your doctor first tells you that you have cancer. It's not uncommon for anyone to shut down mentally once they hear the word "cancer."

There is nothing fair about cancer and no one deserves it. A cancer diagnosis is hard to take and having cancer is not easy. When you find out you have cancer, your personal beliefs and experiences help you figure out what it means to you and how you will handle it.

As you face your own mortality and cope with the many demands of cancer, you may look more closely at your religious beliefs, your **personal and family values, and what's most important** in your life. Accepting the diagnosis and figuring out what cancer will mean in your life is challenging.

After you are diagnosed with this horrible sickness, you may feel shock, disbelief, fear, anxiety, guilt, sadness, grief, depression, anger, and more. Each person may have some or all of these feelings, and each will handle them in a different way.

Your first reaction might be shocking. No one is ever ready to hear that they have cancer. It is normal for people with cancer to wonder why it happened to them or to think life has treated them unfairly. You may not even believe the diagnosis, especially if you don't feel sick.

One might feel afraid. Some people fear cancer itself, while others may be afraid of the cancer treatments. They even wonder how they'll get through those treatments.

You know what is so strange; Liduvina stated that she was feeling guilty. She asked herself many times if she could have noticed her symptoms earlier, or wondered what may have caused the cancer.

She was always wondering if she was exposed to something at home that led to cancer. Sometimes she worried that other members of her family will get cancer, too.

At this time, we do not know what causes most cancers, but a few are known to be hereditary. This means that it is passed from a parent to a child.

If one family member develops it, others in the family may have a higher risk of getting it. This can cause even more concerns for the person newly diagnosed with that deadly disease.

Liduvina was feeling hopeless and very sad most of the time. She used to tell me what would happen to July. I told her many times that I would try to take him to Ponce if he wishes to do so...

She recently told me that it's hard to feel positive and upbeat, especially if the future is uncertain. Just thinking about treatment and the time it will take out of your life can seem like too much to handle. Feelings of sadness or uncertainty may be made worse by your past experiences with cancer.

Sometimes she was very negative. She didn't want to talk to anyone. She told me on one occasion that she could see and feel her body changing. She was trying to make everyone happy. She also began to develop ways to cope with the new, unwanted changes in her life. It took some time for her to become aware of those losses and changes.

It helped her to share her grief with us. There was always someone near her. She sometimes was willing to talk and confide with her mental health professionals. Her feelings needed care too, just like your physical body needs care.

Liduvina was a very wise lady. She was always telling us how she was day by day. She kept on with more advices and her feeling....

She told me that once in a while one might feel angry while other people may not outwardly express their anger and frustration.

Liduvina kept telling me the many strange things about this cancer. That sometimes you may direct your anger toward family members, friends, or health care professionals. It was usually not done on purpose. The cancer patient is only trying to escape their feelings.

She also told that it was hard to let people know that she wasn't angry with anyone. It wasn't her fault. She just needed someone to listen.

On March 2015, I went to her house for a visit. She made a feast for Paul, his mom and me. I bought the dessert. Tio July was so happy to see us.

As always, he was making jokes. Liduvina started telling us about her cancer. Paul's mom told her that she was going into surgery the following week.

She told Liduvina about her breast cancer. Both ladies, whom I love dearly, kept talking about the situation. I just stood there with no word coming out of my mouth. It was so sad listening to them.

All of a sudden, I changed their conversation. We started taking photos of each other. I am glad I did that because now I can share those happy moments.

We finished our photo shoot hour. Liduvina made her famous coffee which I named many years ago, chuchu coffee.

We ended the day with a group hug. It was getting late; therefore, we decided to leave. I stayed in Mayaquez because I was helping Paul with his mother.

Dolores, Paul's mother, went into surgery the following week. I stayed with her after the operation. Also, I made sure she did her follow up checkup.

In May 2015, Liduvina came to visit me in Ponce. She was looking great! Junior, her son, came to see her for mother's day. Liduvina told me that she was going in June to New York.

They were going for a couple of celebrations with the family over there. She kept telling me to join her. I told her that I couldn't leave my father alone.....

Liduvina stayed in New York until September 2015....

Things were not the same after her return. She started getting very sick. Her weigh kept dropping.

When I went to see her I couldn't believe my eyes. She was wasting into nothing. I started talking to her about my childhood. I thank her for always being there for me. There are so many happy memories I shared with her.

I recall one cold winter day in New York. I was operated on my leg. Liduvina called me the night before. She asked me if I needed anything. She was going to see me the next day.

My parents were living in Puerto Rico. I really didn't have anyone to bring me anything. My sister was working; she took off to be with me. Well, I told her that what I wanted was some of her famous coffee and also to bring me some rice, beans and beef stew.

The operation was a success. Liduvina came to see me with my cousin Wanda. They brought the food and I ate the whole thing. When the nurse came to check on me, she told me that I was going to be on a liquid diet for one day.

I told her that I wasn't hungry. The nurse reported everything to the doctor. When the doctor came to see me, he was worried because I didn't want to eat. He told me that if I didn't eat, I was going to stay a couple of days in the hospital. I informed him that I needed to rest and that I would eat everything during dinner.

I was released the following day....

When I was about 6 yrs. old, Liduvina used to take care of my uncle Villen and me. We became her shadow. She just got married with my uncle Julio. She was left in Puerto Rico alone, because my uncle was in the service.

Liduvina took Villen and me everywhere. We went to the river and the beach. Her parents used to live in Guayanila, PR. Their house was right next to the beach. It was so beautiful around that area. There was always something to do because Liduvina had a very large family. There were kids all over the place. We had a lot of family outing in Guayanilla and in Ponce. I do miss those days.

Liduvina's parents were very sweet. Don Angel, Liduvina's father, was always waiting for us every Sunday morning. He used to tell me not to play with the chickens because that was going to be our lunch. His wife, Doña Luz, used to twist those chickens' neck and within minutes, the chickens were in the pot.

While living in New York, we spent many holidays with Liduvina and the rest of the family. They had three kids, Junior, Sandra and Wanda. Wanda died in January 1981.

Liduvina suffered a lot when Wanda died. The whole family was suffering during that time. Wanda was truly a wonderful daughter, cousin, friend etc. She was always happy. Heaven received a cute and adorable angel.

When Liduvina returned to Puerto Rico in September 2015, her doctor told her that she only had a couple of weeks to live. It was devastating seeing her sick day after day.

My sister came to see her just before Christmas. Liduvina got so happy when she saw my sister and me. We sat next to her and talk for hours. Liduvina didn't want us to leave, but we had to.

I went to see her couple of times after Christmas. My uncle called me on April 29, 2016. He told me that it was time. Liduvina had just a couple of hours. I called one of my cousins and we all went to Isabela that very same day.

Liduvina couldn't talk, but she was aware of everyone around her.

There were a lot of people in her bedroom. She kept crying that her body was hurting. It was impossible not to cry. I left the room so that no one could see my tears. When everyone went to the dining room to eat, I was alone with her and my uncle.

At this point, I had flashbacks of my dying mother. I didn't see my uncle. I saw my father sitting there holding my mother's hand. I had to hold my tears because I didn't want my uncle to notice my sad face. I started making jokes.

I asked Liduvina who was her honey bun. She replied very softly, July. I also asked her, who is the love of her life, she replied once again, July. I told Liduvina that she can leave because July would be taken care of by the whole family.

I didn't want to leave my uncle, but I couldn't stay either. My father was in Ponce and I have to make sure that he ate and took his medication.

Every day my aunt Lucy called me to tell me about Liduvina. My aunt Lucy was going home and my other aunt Lolin stayed. My family really came very close during those days.

By May 2, 2016, aunt Lolin returned to PR with my aunt Norma. They stayed endless nights without any sleep taking care of Liduvina…

On May 7, 2016, my aunt Norma called. She just said that Liduvina died at about 7:20 a.m. I got the call at 7:25 a.m.

Even though I knew that day was going to come, I wasn't ready. One is never ready to accept any death in the family.

You know, Liduvina had two funerals. We had a wake in Guayanilla on May 10, 2016. My uncle July was happy because we were there to give him moral support. He told all his friends that we were his family.

The following day, Liduvina's body was place on a horse and buggy. We went the beach where she used to spend her happy moments. There were plenty of people there.

As we approached the seaport, many boats started blowing their horns. We got off the car and stood beside my aunt Lucy. All of the sudden, my body started to shake. I started moving my arms and feet. I didn't want anyone to notice what was going on with me. Then, I was feeling better. We walked to the car speechless.

The Liduvina was then taken to Isabela for another viewing. She was buried in Isabela on 12 May 2016.

Rest in peace my dear Liduvina.

Chapter 28

My Best Friend

Who do you consider your best friend?

It is very simple. A best friend is the one that calls you and makes sure that you are doing well.

When I was working, I had lots of friends. I went to numerous parties. I had no problem driving in the snow, in the dark, or in a bright sunny day.

Now, I cannot do favors, drive people around and so on. I have problems with my vision and I only drive short distances and in the early morning hours.

In some occasions, I start driving and have to stop or return home. The sun is very bright or the sky starts turning gray. My condition is really bad. My doctor told me to start making plans for the future. I will never give up.

I went to see my optometrist and received new eye drops. I can see much better these past few days. I won't be going for another eye operation.

During those bad days, is when you know who are your true friends.

Well, now that I am retired and can only say that I still have one friend that is always there for me. His name is Paul Chique.

We know each other for more than fifteen years…

Paul calls me every morning to make sure that I am going to the gym or ready to do my chores. He lives very far from me. That is the reason he calls....

At the present time, Paul is taking care of his mother. She is not doing well. I am there if she needs me, but I cannot go to her side all the time. I am also taking care of my father. So both Paul and I have our hands full.

Let me tell you why I enjoy Paul's company. We both have the same interest in music, art and movies. He is an artist and had done a lot of the jewelry I own.

Sometimes we go to the beach and he starts drawing something. I just look at him and begin writing. It is so funny because sometimes I wrote about the same thing he just drew and we start laughing.

When it comes to cooking, he is the best. I just tell him to come over and we will invent something in the kitchen. He makes great egg rolls and Chinese rice.

The other day he came to the rescues…

My uncle Kike was in the hospital. Kike was the one I used to call when I needed a driver. He was always there for me. I feel so bad because I cannot help him. It has been raining for almost three days straight; therefore, I cannot drive….

On that particular morning, when I needed help, Paul came to my house. He helped with my house work, prepared breakfast for my dad while I fed the dogs. We took my car for inspection and went to visit my uncle at the hospital.

Paul always makes my day. When I am sad, he would start singing. I just laugh because sometimes he sounds awful…

You know today we took an IQ test. We both scored 160!!!! I know we are smart because we do stuff that normal people have problems doing.

Everyone keeps telling us that we should get marry. My answer is always no. The minute two people start living under the same roof, the fun is gone.

There is never dull moment when we are together. I know that if we get marry, we would stop being the best of friends.

Paul knows that I am here for him and I know that he is always there for me. Thank you for being my best friend.

In the following, I am going to narrate a story that happened to me as I was growing up. This will explain why I am happy the way I am now. It will also explain that it isn't easy finding best friends.

There was a time when I had a lot of friends. I wasn't a bit shy. I was really popular or I thought I was. I always had someone to share secrets and laughs. All through high school, though, I didn't slip in and out of friendships.

Why because I was in the honor roll. I helped my so-called friends with their schoolwork.

When it came time to go to college, I was quite nervous. I was going to be rooming with someone I didn't know. I was going to live in a town about 800 miles away from home.

There wouldn't be a single person I knew in town. I had no idea how I was going to make friends in this new environment.

The first week of classes, something happened. It changed my life forever. In my English class, I was asked to talk a little about my life. I told everyone where I came from.

I spoke about the place I called home. I express myself very well. If I was nervous, it didn't show. I shared a lot of information.

As always, there was a final question for each student. It was always the same: "What is your goal for this class?" Now, most of the students said it was to get a good grade, pass the class or something similar, but for some reason, I said something entirely different. I said that my goal was to make just one good friend.

While most of the students sat in silence, one student came to me and held out his hand. He then introduced himself. He asked me if I would be his friend.

The whole room was silent. All eyes focused on us and the hand extended just in front of me. I smiled and stretched my hand out to take his and a friendship was formed. It was a friendship that lasted all through college. It was a friendship that turned into a romance. It was a friendship that brought two people together forever....

During that time, I was happy yes, however, one thing really mess everything up. There was a war and my best friend was drafted. He was killed in Vietnam and I never had a chance to tell him thank you for all the good and bad times we shared together.

Many years went by and I never forgot my friend. I met someone else and we got married. We got a divorced because of so many differences in our lives....

After I graduated from college, I started working in a law firm. I made friends right away; however, there was one girl that I do prefer to keep her name anonymous. We became extremely close, but soon I figured out unfortunately, that we weren't as close as I thought we were....

Before our friendship ended, she came over to my house frequently. We spent a lot of quality time together. We always talks about men we found attractive. We also talked about our relationships.

Everything was great. We got along just fine we had what I thought was a strong bond. We enjoyed each other's company. We had fun together.

Then one day, everything changed. She came over after work. I was putting together a presentation assigned by our supervisor. I was happy to see my friend because the following day we were going to present our project to the whole staff.

All of a sudden, I received a call from my sister. I took the call and went to another room to talk. I was gone for about half hour. When I came back, I noticed my "friend" was gone. I was very confused. I did not expect that. I remember thinking to myself.

"She could have at least said I am leaving or just good bye." When I was ready to go to bed, I noticed that my presentation was gone.

That night I couldn't sleep. I remember turning on my bed... Just thinking to myself... "She could have stolen my presentation. She's my "friend" right? Or was she?" Later that day I went to work. The whole office congratulated her for the outstanding presentation.

My supervisor was angry at me because I showed up late and wasn't there to be part of the presentation. I did say anything and left the room.

I went looking for my friend. I confronted her about my presentation. I told that I have worked very hard on my own and she got the credit. My boss thinks that you did it all alone.

She told me "I'm your friend. I would never do that to you." So unfortunately I took her word. The following day, my supervisor went to her office and to my surprise, she came back and showed me the whole presentation. My friend forgot to edit the work and half of the presentation had my name on it....

I was in shock! I just did not know what to say or how to feel. It then later struck me that it actually happened. I felt lost and confused, hurt, used, and betrayed. I thought I could trust my so call friend.

I do not regret meeting her because it showed me that even the people you care about will betray you.

I learned a lesson that helped me a lot in the future. I learned that you can have acquaintances, but those could never be real friends.

Chapter 29

My kids have paws

You know, people ask me, when I first meet them, if I have any children. My answer is always the same. Yes, I have three children. The only difference from yours is that my children are four legged and have paws.

If you want to cause a commotion in a place where animal and human behavior is studied, all you have to do is claim that your dog loves you. Disbelievers, opponents, and even some passionate supporters will pour out into the halls to argue that statement.

Among the skeptics you will find the veterinarian Fred Metzger, of Pennsylvania State University. He claims that dogs probably don't feel love in the typical way humans do.

Dogs make investments in human beings because it works for them. They have something to gain from putting so-called emotions out there.

Metzger believes that dogs "love" us only as long as we continue to reward their behaviors with treats and attention. For most dog owners, however, there is little doubt that dogs can truly love people.

I want you to read the following story about a dog named Rocky and his owner Rita. They were from the Finger Lakes region of New York State, near Rochester. Rocky was 65-pound Boxer, classically colored with a chestnut brown coat and a white blaze on his chest.

At the time of this story, Rocky was three years old. Rita was 11 yrs. old. Rocky had been given to Rita when he was ten weeks old. She immediately bonded with him.

She used to pet him and fed him. Rita taught Rocky many basic commands. She even let him sleep on her bed. Whenever she was not in school, the two were always together and within touching distance.

The whole family would often fondly refer to the pair as "R and R." Rita was a very shy girl; therefore, as the dog grew, he gave her a sense of security.

When Rocky was next to her she felt confident enough to meet new people. Rita wasn't afraid to go to unfamiliar places when Rocky was around.

Rocky took on the role, not only of a friend, but also of defender. Also, when encountering strangers, he would often deliberately stand in front of Rita, as a sort of protective barrier. He seemed to be without fear.

Once, Rita was going shopping. She was about to enter a store when there were two large men dressed in biker outfits already ahead of her.

They burst out of the door, yelling at the shopkeeper, and nearly knocking Rita over. Rocky rushed forward putting himself between the frightened girl and the two threatening men. He braced himself and gave a low rumbling growl that carried such menace that the two men backed off.

Rocky always gave Rita full protection. There was, however, one weakness in Rocky's armor. It was a fear of water that was so life-threatening that it was almost pathological. Boxers are not strong swimmers in any event, and are often shy of the water.

Rocky's fears began since his puppyhood. At the age of seven weeks, he was sold to a family with an adolescent child. The boy had emotional problems and acted as if the attention given to the new puppy somehow meant that he was less important.

The boy, in a jealous rage, put the puppy in a pillow case, knotted the top and threw it into a lake. Fortunately, the boy's father saw the incident and managed to retrieve the terrified puppy before it drowned. The father reprimanded the boy and returned to the house.

The next day, the horrified father saw his son standing waist-deep in the lake trying to drown the struggling puppy by holding him under water. This time Rocky was rescued and returned to the breeder for his own safety.

All those early traumas made water the only thing that Rocky truly feared. When he came close to a body of water, he would try to pull back and seemed emotionally distressed.

Every time Rita would go swimming, he would pace along the shore trembling and whimpering. He would watch her intently and would not relax until she returned to dry land.

One late afternoon, Rita's mother took R and R to an upscale shopping area. It was located along the edge of a lake. It featured a short wooden boardwalk which was built along the shore over a sharp embankment that was 20 or 30 feet above the surface of the water.

Rita started walking along the boardwalk. She was enjoying the sounds of water. It was then that a boy on a bicycle skidded on the damp wooden surface, hitting Rita. She was hit at an angle which propelled her through an open section of the guard rail.

She let out a shriek of pain and fear. She hurled outward and down, hitting the water face down. She was floating there and unmoving.

Rita's mother was at the entrance of a store a hundred feet or so away. She rushed to the railing shouting for help. Rocky was already there, looking at the water, trembling in fear.

He was making sounds that seemed to be a combination of barks, whimpers, and yelps all rolled into one. We can never know what went through that dog's mind as he stood looking at the water. The water was the one thing that truly terrified him and that had nearly taken his life twice.

Now, here was a frightening body of water that seemed about to harm his little mistress. Whatever he was thinking, his love for Rita seemed to overpower his fear. He leapt out through the same open space in the rail and plunged into the water…

One can thank the genetic programming that allowed the dog to swim without any prior practice. He immediately went to Rita and grabbed her by a shoulder strap on her dress. This caused her to roll over so that her face was out of the water.

Rita gagged and coughed. Despite her dazed state she reached out and managed to cinch her hand in Rocky's collar. All this was happening while the dog struggled to swim toward the shore. Fortunately the water was calm.

They were not far from shore; therefore, Rocky quickly reached a depth where his feet were on solid ground. He dragged Rita until her head was completely out of the water.

He then stood beside her, licking her face, while he continued to tremble and whine. It would be several minutes before human rescuers would make it down the steep rocky embankment.

This incident stated that if it has not been for Rocky, they surely would have arrived too late. Rita and her family believe that it was only the big dog's love for the little girl that caused him to take what he must have considered a life-threatening action.

This certainly casts doubt on Dr. Metzger's theory that dogs don't love us but act only out of self-interest. Why should Rocky behave in a way that he certainly felt would risk his life?

Surely, if he was evaluating the costs and benefits of his actions then he would have known that, even in Rita's absence, the rest of the family would be around to feed him and take care of needs.

Marc Bekoff, a behavioral biologist at the University of Colorado, has a different interpretation. He stated that dogs are social animals. All social animals need emotions as means of communication.

For example, you need to know when to back off if another animal is growling. More importantly, however, emotions keep the social group together and motivate individuals to protect and support each other.

Bekoff concluded that strong emotion is one of the foundations of social behavior. It is also the basis of the connection between individuals in any social group, whether it is a pack, a family or just a couple in love.

Recent research has even identified some of the chemicals associated with feelings of love in humans. These include hormones such as oxytocin, which seem to help people form emotional bonds with each other.

One of the triggers that cause oxytocin to be released is gentle physical touching, such as stroking. Dogs also produce oxytocin, and one of our common ways of interacting with dogs is to gently pet them. This is an action that probably releases this hormone associated with bonding.

If dogs as social animals have an evolutionary need for close emotional ties, they have the chemical mechanisms associated with loving; it makes sense to assume that they are capable of loving, as we are.

Rocky's fear of the water was absolute, and never did abate. He continued to avoid it for the rest of his life. No one ever saw him so much as place a foot in the lake again. No one, at least not Rita or her family, ever doubted his love for her.

He lived long enough to see an event occur which would not have happened had he not cared for her as much as he did.

When Rita graduated from high school, she posed for a photo in her cap and gown. Beside her, sat a now much older Boxer.

The smiling girl had an arm around the dog, and her hand was cinched in his collar, as it was the day that Rocky clearly showed her just how much he loved her.

I told you this story because I do believe dogs can love a human being.

I always had dogs. When I was a kid, at one time, we had a dog, a cat and a bird. The dog belonged to me. The cat was just there. He had no official owner. My sister owned the bird. We were taught at an early age to love animals....

At the present time, I have three dogs. They are Blackie, Titi and Pica. Those dogs follow me everywhere. There is never a dull moment in my house. I taught them to dance. Whenever they hear music, they run towards me. They know when I am happy because of the music I play.

I call them my little angels. Why are they my little angels? Well, when my mom was alive, they took care of her. They knew when my mom wasn't doing well. I know they miss her because sometimes I call her name and they look around for her.

Now, I live with my dad and three dogs. My father has so many ailment s that I don't know where to begin my second story.

Let me tell you one scenario where the dogs saved my father's life…

Before I retired, I used to get up a 5:00 am. I used to prepare my parents breakfast and their lunch.

On one particular day, I noticed that my dad wasn't well. I couldn't depend on my mom because she had Alzheimer.

Before I left for work, I asked my dad if he was feeling better. He told me that he was fine.

I reported to work, however, my mind wasn't there. I was thinking about my parents. I gave my 8:00 class and then I was on my break.

I tried calling home and there was no answer. I waited a couple of minutes and to my surprise, my neighbor was calling me. She told me that the dogs were barking for a long time.

She began calling my parents and there was no answer. The dogs were making very strange sound. I thank her and decided to go home When I got home, I found my mother crying on top of my father. He had fallen and was unconscious. The dogs stopped barking, however, they were making strange sounds. I went to the kitchen and prepared malt for my dad. I gave it to him. My dad had no idea what had happened. I told him that his sugar level dropped and he was unconscious.

My dogs saved my father's life….

There were many incidents involving my parents and my dogs…

Since my mom's death, I have to make sure my dad is well taken care. The dogs are always on the alert. If my father falls, they will go and get me. It is strange, but I do depend on my three legged kids. Train your dogs and they will be you friends for the rest of their life.

Chapter 30

Life After Retirement

When someone is getting closer to retire, a lot of questions come to mind. What will I do when I retire? Is my income good enough to survive? Etc...

For a lot of people, the key to a happy and fulfilling retirement is simple: staying busy. Unfortunately, when planning for your retire-ment, is not easy.

Some folks focus only on finances, and fail to think about, or plan for, how they will spend their time.

I started planning for my retirement very early in life. Some of my friends used to tell me why worry about retirement activities so ear-ly in life. Retirement is years, or even decades, away. I just simply smile.

In my opinion, I wanted to count on developing new interest and involve myself in something constructive after the age of 65. I am glad I did because if I didn't, it would have been a bore. I would have been a depressed old lady...

THIS IS WHAT I DID WHEN I RETIRED.

The first thing I did was to join a gym. I retired on May 15, 2014 and I started my gym classes the following day.

I got a personal trainer because I was really over weight and com-pletely out of shape. My trainers, Christian Quiles and Adys Delgado helped me a lot. They started me off with a very strict balanced diet. They explained the importance of eating five meals a day.

I used to skip meals and never really had any good eating habits. I learned from both trainers that in order to lose weight, you have to be very discipline not only in the exercise sessions, but also at home.

I am happy to say that I lost over 85 lbs. I feel great and look great. Thanks to both of my personal trainers.

Well guess what? I also made new of friends at the gym.

Yes there is much more than fitness at a gym/fitness center. It's a great community social center.

Attending gym/fitness center can provide a fun and relaxing atmosphere. In addition to all the equipment and services available to you, one can really make friends.

I met Mai Rojo Gaa, Lisa Collazo, Margarita Febus, Roxanne De Jesus, Maria Jimenez, Ines, Gaby, Nancy, Virgen and Michelle to name a few.

Let me tell you a bit about Mai Rojo Gaa. She is really a very special lady. She always has kind words about everyone at the gym. Every time she sees me she tells that I am doing great.

Mai also gives great parties. She has a wonderful family. She has two boys. They are very polite and friendly. When there is a get together at her house, her husband always makes sure that everyone is having fun.

I repeat once again that one of the best advantages to belonging to gym/fitness center is the opportunity to develop friendships and re-patronships with fellow members and staff. Everyone is always offering you encouragement, humor, and motivation.

I almost forgot to mention Julio Ortiz. He is the director at the gym where I go. He helped me a great deal. I was always very sad because I just loss my mother. He made sure that I was working out and also making friends. Now, he just greets me with a big smile because he knows that I am doing just fine.

Diana Maldonado is another outstanding trainer that helped me.. Julio and Diana are awesome.

Renovating not only my life, but also my house

In January 2016, I contacted Alfonso Vega. He and his church members came to the rescue. They began renovating my whole house. It took several months, but it was worth it. I am very happy to have met Fonso's friends. I call them my little angels. Those guys worked very hard to make me a dream house.

Now that I am retired, I have the time to go to a gym, make new friends, write poems, and work in my garden. Before, I didn't have any time to do a thing. I was working, but I was also killing myself.

I thank God every day for my blessings. All I have to say is that there is life after retirement.

Chapter 31

Afterword

The main reason I wrote this book is to remind people of their family values. I still think on how my parents raised me. They taught me to respect my grandparents, uncles and aunts. They were part of me as I was growing up.

Family values consist of ideas passed down from generation to generation. It boils down to the philosophy of how you want to live your family life.

There are three traditional basic tasks in life that people look at as family values. They have been described as work, play and love. There are many activities that fall under these categories that define our values.

All of them are important and it takes work to balance these tasks. However, we often get caught up in work and other activities and neglect play and love.

Many times we work hard because we are investing in our career goals, material things and financial rewards. Yet without a balanced life of incorporating play and having loving relationships, our lives become stressful, overwhelming and unsatisfying.

Traditionally people define their values as stating that the family comes first, however, they find themselves with very little time or energy left over for spending time with the family.

What does family time mean to you?

This may mean something different to each member of your family. How about a family reunion to provide an opportunity for all members to come together?

It is easy to get caught up in activities and schedules which leaves little time for the family. Also, family meeting is a great opportunity to prioritize the things your family values and establish traditions. Schedule a reunion or meeting at least once a month to determine your family values.

I will always treasure what I had and will never forget them. We had strong family ties; therefore, we grew up helping each other.

My message to all is to never forget your origin. When I was in New York as a child, all I wanted was to return to my island. I returned to my place of birth. I brought with me a lot of knowledge and wisdom. I passed it on to all the students I taught in Puerto Rico. My mission was accomplished...

References

1. Real Cédula de 1789 "para el comercio de Negros"
2. Rouse, Irving. The Tainos: Rise and Decline of the People Who Greeted Columbus ISBN 0-300-05696-6.
3. Mahaffy, Cheryl (January 28, 2006). "Vieques Island - What lies beneath". Edmonton Journal. Retrieved February 11, 2006.
4. Figueroa, Ivonne (July 1996). "Taínos". Retrieved March 20, 2006.
5. Pedro Torres. "The Dictionary of the Taíno Language". Taino Inter-Tribal Council Inc. Retrieved February 11, 2006.
6. Brau, Salvador (1894). Puerto Rico y su historia: investigaciones críticas (in Spanish). Valencia, Spain: Francisco Vives Moras. pp. 96–97.
7. Vicente Yañez Pinzón is considered the first appointed governor of Puerto Rico, but he never arrived on the island.
8. PROCLAMATION presented by Dennis O. Freytes, MPA, MHR, BBA, Chair/Facilitator, 500TH Florida Discovery Council Round Table, American Veteran, Community Servant, VP NAUS SE Region; Chair Hispanic Achievers Grant Council
9. Mari, Brenda A. (April 22, 2005). "The Legacy of Añasco: Where the Gods Come to Die". Puerto Rico Herald. Archived from the original on April 27, 2006. Retrieved March 1, 2006.
10. "Taino Tribal Census Registration: A Record of Hope and Survival". La Salita Cafe. Retrieved 28 November 2014.

11. Jones, W.A. "Porto Rico". Catholic Encyclopedia. Retrieved March 4, 2006.

12. "Religion". Puerto Rico: A Guide to the Island of Boriquén. Federal Writers Project. 1940. Retrieved March 6, 2006.

13. Hispanic Firsts, by, Nicolas Kanellos, publisher Visible Ink Press; ISBN 0-7876-0519-0; p.40

14. "La Fortaleza/San Juan National Historic Site, Puerto Rico". National Park Service. Archived from the original on February 8, 2006. Retrieved March 1, 2006.

15. Miller, Paul G. (1947).Historias de Puerto Rico,221–237.

16. "The Life of Sir Francis Drake". July 20, 2004. Retrieved March 1, 2006.

17. The exact number of ships and troops is presently uncertain. The number of ships varies from 60 to 64 ships and the number of troops varies from 7,000 to 13,000. No exact number of ships is given by British accounts. For more information see Alonso, María M., and The Eighteenth Century Caribbean & The British Attack on Puerto Rico in 1797 ISBN 1-881713-20-2.

18. Alonso, María M. "Chapter XIV - Abercromby's Siege" (PDF). The Eighteenth Century Caribbean & The British Attack on Puerto Rico in 1797. Retrieved February 28, 2006.

19. Caro Costas, Aida R. (1980). Antología de Lecturas de Historia de Puerto Rico (Siglos XV-XVIII), p. 467.

20. Abbad y Lasierra, Iñigo. Historia Geográfica, Civil y Política de Puerto Rico (in Spanish). S.l.: Univ Of Puerto Rico Pr. ISBN 0-8477-0800-4.

21. Interview of Thomas Ellingwood Fortin, Producer, NEW ALBION PICTURES

22. Words from Pres. Ronald Reagan

23. "Aspectos politicos en Puerto Rico: 1765–1837" (in Spanish). Retrieved March 4, 2006.

24. 150th. Anniversary of the Foundation of Arroyo, Puerto Rico

25. NY/Latino Journal; Taking the PE Out of PRT; by: Rafael Merino Cortes; July 20, 2006

26. "Slave revolts in Puerto Rico: conspiracies and uprisings, 1795-1873"; by: Guillermo A. Baralt; Publisher Markus Wiener Publishers; ISBN 1-55876-463-1, ISBN 978-1-55876-463-7

27. Grose, Howard B., Advance in the Antilles; the new era in Cuba and Porto Rico, OCLC 1445643 (These clauses included that slaves were required to continue working for three more years and that the owners would be compensated 35 million pesetas per slave.)

28. Negroni, Héctor Andrés (1992). Historia militar de Puerto Rico (in Spanish). Societal Stately Quinto Centenario. ISBN 978-84-7844-138-9.

29. "Chronology of Puerto Rico in the Spanish-American War". Library of Congress. Retrieved March 10, 2006.

30. This legislature consisted of a Council of Administration with eight elected and seven appointed members, and a Chamber of Representatives with one member for every 25,000 inhabitants.

31. Strategy as Politics by Jorge Rodriguez Beruff; Publisher: La Editorial; Universidad de Puerto Rico; page 7; ISBN 978-0-8477-0160-5

32. "The World of 1898: The Spanish-American War". Hispanic Division, Library of Congress. Retrieved 2008-08-03.

33. "Military Government in Puerto Rico". Library of Congress. Retrieved March 26, 2006.

34. Blackburn Moreno, Ronald (February 2001). "Brief

35. Chronology of Puerto Rico" (PDF). ASPIRA Association, Inc. Archived from the original (PDF) on February 17, 2006. Retrieved February 11, 2006.

36. My aunt Luz E. Pagan Rodriguez,
My uncle Ramon L. Pagan Rodriguez
My father Juan J. Pagan Rodriguez
My Grandmother Ceferina Figueroa Bello

My Grandmother Guadalupe Rodriguez Quiles
Told me many stories about Puerto Rico
& my FAMILY

About the Author

Norma Iris Pagan Morales was born in Ponce, Puerto Rico. She comes from a very lovable family. Her parents, Juan Jose Pagan Rodriguez, and Digna Morales Figueroa, now deceased, always helped her with her projects as a writer and teaching career.

Norma had three siblings, Adelin Milagros Pagan Morales, Juan Jose Pagan Morales, and Julio Manuel Pagan Morales. Julio Manuel Pagan Morales died on September 19, 1998, and My dear sister Adelin Milagros Pagan Morales died on February 17, 2023.

Norma did all her academic studies in New York City, Puerto Rico, and Canada. She worked in the City of New York Police Department. As an Educator, she worked in New York City Bd. of Education as an English Teacher, in Puerto Rico Bd. of Education as an English teacher and in the Puerto Rico Army National.

She has teaching certifications for English as a Second Language and Teaching English as a Foreign Language.

She had published thirteen books: Proud of My Puerto Rican Bequest, ¿Porque Soy Boricua? Poemas del Alma, Art in Written Form, A Baffling Short Stories Collection, On Job in the Big Apple, Puerto Rican Soldiers Serving with Pride, Nature's Rage in the Caribbean, Boricua de Pura Cepa, You are the One, The Unfaithfuls, Christopher Columbus and Violence in the City.